New Leash on Life

By Anne Mallore

To Marc,
May you be always
blessed with love
and good times!
Much love
Anne Mallore

D1523082

Copyright © 2014 by Anne Mallore.

All Rights Reserved. No part of this book may be used or reproduced by any means, graphic, electronic, mechanical including photocopying, recording, taping or by any information storage retrieval system without written permission of the publisher except in cases where brief quotations embodies in articles and reviews.

Published by Divine Phoenix
Divine Phoenix Books may be ordered by www.divinephoenixbooks.com
Graphic Design: Chris Moebs

ISBN-13: 978-0-9853915-0-8
ISBN-10: 0985391502

First Edition, June 2014

Printed in the United States of America

Preface

I wrote this book with the hope that others will find the courage to fight on and not give up when facing unimaginable circumstances. I want the reader to take from the story a will to continue on with the journey of life, to not give up, and to trust that God has a plan for you. The path given may not be the path you chose, but the one that will be the most gratifying in the long run.

Many great people have failed before they reached their true calling, but they persevered. Find what you truly love to do in life, and incorporating that into a means to survive, you will find peace. Contentment also comes with the job. Self-worth is reaffirmed and faith restored. Listening with your heart can bring you there. Don't be afraid. Choose a path of self-belief and step over your fears.

Everything truly does happen for a reason. We are as we are supposed to be right now. There are no coincidences. Too many people fall into despair, or give up the fight before they even give themselves a chance to taste victory. Be brave! Know you aren't alone in your struggles. Everyone faces trials in their life. Be strong, don't give up. Hang in there! In your darkest moments, the sun still shines and isn't that a blessing in itself?

- Anne Mallore

Dedication

This book is dedicated to my husband, Carmen. He pushed me to write what I felt and believed that I could write something that people would actually want to read.   Thank you for your love, resilience, and for your commitment to Wags. I used to be the rock, I passed that on to you. Thank you for building my dream and making it wag.

Also, to the best two things I ever created, my boys, CJ and Sammy. Thank you for being my heart and soul. I love you with all that I am. Thank you for riding the wave, especially when it gets rough, and for all of the hugs even when you gave them up reluctantly!

For my Dad and Mom, for your support, love and gentle healing. I thank you with all of my heart! I am so blessed to be your daughter!

For my "Angels on Earth", "Grace", you know who you are, Bonnie, and "Dr. Nancy" for giving me home, Longboat Key and sanity, in that order. But, most of all, for your friendship. I could never have survived without you! Remember, "small kindnesses"...

For all of my beloved pets, Woody, Princess Kitty, Wiley, Lola and Clark. No medicine works better than being loved by a pet.

Acknowledgements

To Laura Ponticello. Without your encouragement, I would never have written my story. It has been cathartic, cleansing, healing and, at times, very difficult. I am so glad Bunny dragged you in!

To our former attorney, Bill. Thank you. "I couldn't have done this without you" sounds so trite and sarcastic. Honestly, I don't mean it that way. My thank you is truly heartfelt. I know I told you in the note, shit happens. We are going to be great. We are right where we are supposed to be. Blessings and good wishes to you and yours.

To all of my guests and your families. Thank you for choosing Wags. I so appreciate all the support, hugs, thank you notes, cookies, and treats we get from you all!

"Try to be a rainbow in someone's cloud."
    -   Maya Angelou

Peace is contentment. A leaf caught on a breeze. A feather drifting slowly to ground. Quiet is not essential to peace, nor is solitude. Peace is a state of being no matter where you are and flows out of you as confidence. Pure joy is uncontainable. Joy shows in every step you take, everything you do.

"You smile all the time!" Do I? I was unaware. I know I used to, people told me that often. Better than being miserable. I would think at times that people would take it to mean that there wasn't a lot going on up in my head, but in reality, there is. The face you wear is really an exterior image of what is going on in your head.

I show my feelings on my face, all of us do. Some people don't like the true face to be seen, because the face is too raw and honest. We don't control that. Emotional truth is deeper seeded than that. It is so obvious when someone puts on a false face, one to show the world. The true being lurks just beyond the false face and oozes out to show the true face.

Smugness is the worst. I feel bad for the face that is hiding behind a smug look. There is fear, lack of confidence, anger, hate or jealousy in a smug face. Maybe a combination of all, but it is a sad face, none the less. Happy is the one that can show his true face. There is no fear in a true face, so the true face can smile.

Introduction

My name is Anne Mallore. I am the owner of Wag's Pet Center. I have always had a profound love of animals and worked for years in the pet industry. We opened Wags in August of 2007 as a means to survive and to fulfill a dream. I am asked frequently how we got into this business and how we started. No one knows the whole story. Some think they do. They may know part, but not really. That is why I'm writing this book, so I can tell my story.

I know that we are not unique in our experiences. I read about devastation like this all the time. Each case is unique as to how it is handled. We chose to survive, no, to thrive, to pick ourselves up and press ahead. The alternative was not attractive at all, and not an option.

Simply put, we had a very successful business before building Wags. We did not, however, surround ourselves with the right people and we suffered the consequences as a result. We delegated where we should not have delegated. We misplaced our trust. We failed. This caused a ripple that engulfed us and over took us.

We lost everything that we had, our vehicles, possessions, our home, and our sense of self. Our loss is a death and a death that took its toll. We also lost some of our closest friends. It felt like we had a plague and no one wanted to be around us for fear of our bad luck. That was really hard. Heartbreaking. We were mortally wounded, but we survived. The love of family and shear will brought us through difficult hurdles, and faith. If you don't have faith, there is no hope and without hope, there is nothing.

Chapter 1

My faith came from my family. I was raised with my two sisters, Susan and Mary, older sisters and a younger brother Tom. We are 13 months apart, my brother and I, and we were always together. He was my best friend. My mom says that whenever one of us got sick, the other would help in the healing so we could get back to play again.

Where ever you saw Tommy you would see Teeney. That was my nickname when I was little, because I was little. Angel Anne when I was good, Terrible Teeney when I wasn't so good. We had a great childhood. My parents worked very hard to provide us with everything essential to grow up into productive human beings.

Dad worked his nine to five job and then "moonlighted', worked a second job, so we never went without what we needed. My Mom was a secretary at our

Middle School when we were kids, and later became an executive secretary at a construction company. Every summer we took a vacation as a family. My parents would save all year for whatever adventure. Those trips were great.

The Bay of Fundy and when we were drenched by rain in our leaky tent is a great memory. And the fog! We swam in the bay and walked the beach when the tide went out. Such an incredible place. Cape Cod, and all of its small villages. We were invited to stay in the home of the owners of a motel my parents had booked. It was lovely.

We visited Provincetown and did not realize as a kid, what a vacation mecca for the gay community that the locale had become. It was beautiful, vibrant, and so friendly! I don't think my parents had any idea about Provincetown's emerging identity either. I really don't think they cared. I do think they were a bit surprised to see so many fabulous people in one place! They don't judge people. It's "live and let live". They passed that trait on to me. Everyone we met was so nice to us! We had a great time.

We camped in Vermont, New Hampshire, and Maine. The rugged Maine coastline was spectacular, the mountains in Vermont and New Hampshire, breathtaking. We camped at beautiful Lake Kandle in New Jersey.

It was so much fun. The journey to our destination was always part of the adventure. My sisters and I had "toe socks", multicolored socks that were like gloves for the feet. We would hang them out the open tailgate window for our amusement and that of whomever happened to be behind us. Oh, and seat belts? Nope. We just sat in the back-facing seat or folded the seat down and laid on blankets.

We were four kids in a Country Squire station wagon who had the time of our lives. I remember one adventure when we stopped and got ice cream. My brother Tom's ice cream cone was dripping and we girls were yelling at him to lick the cone before the ice cream hit the seat. He lifted the cone up only to smash it into the roof of the car! What a mess. No worries, the car cleaned up just fine!

My parents shared their world with us and it was wonderful. We weren't perfect kids, but my parents knew they could take us anywhere and we wouldn't embarrass them. We respected them; they deserved our respect by setting a proper example. We knew without a doubt that we were loved. I always knew that my parents were there for me and loved me and my siblings unconditionally.

I was raised in the Catholic Faith. My dad had an uncle and cousins that were Catholic Priests so I grew up with the knowledge that Priests are people, not just men of the cloth. When my Dad was 12, he took a train from New York to Big Stone City, South Dakota to spend the summer with his father's brother, Father George. Dad was an altar boy for Father George at his parish there. It was 1945. My dad recently told me that when the end of World War Two was announced, he, along with Father George, went up and rang the bells in the Church to announce the news.

Father George was beloved by his parish and respected by his peers. After spending twenty-one years in Big Stone City, Father George was asked to go to Dell Rapids, South Dakota to build the new St. Mary's church there. He worked diligently on the church and as a result, the experience impacted him.

Father was there a little over a year when he passed away on October 25, 1951. He was only fifty-four years old. Some say the constant work and stress of building a new church was to blame, and Father George's death came as a shock to his church community.

I grew up with our cousins, Father Frederick and his brother Father Andrew, as a staple in our lives. Fathers Fred and Andrew, their brother Ed and sister Marie, had been raised by my great grandparents as their own parents had been killed in an automobile accident when the children were young.

My great grandparents, George and Olivia, took the train to California to retrieve their niece and nephews, Andrew, Water, Marie and Ed. They brought them back to Bayonne New Jersey to live with their three children, George, Henry and Anne. I'm sure it wasn't easy for any of them. The four children lost their parents and were moved to the opposite coast.

There were four new mouths to feed in George and Olivia's house. They made their combined family life work and all of the children thrived. George, Andrew and Walter went on to Seminary School. They were ordained Fathers George, Andrew, and Frederick. Walter was the only one that didn't keep his given name when ordained.

He chose Frederick when he received the Sacrament of Holy Orders. His family still called him Walter. Marie, Henry and Ed went on to have families of their own, Henry being my father's father. All of the children remained very close and involved in each other's lives. When Father George passed away, Father Andrew served as deacon and Father Fred served as sub-deacon, assisting the Bishop of Sioux Falls for Father George's funeral mass.

Summers were wonderful for me and my siblings. Many trips were made to Bayonne, New Jersey and Aunt Anne's house. Frequently, Father Fred or Father Andrew would arrive to take us to dinner. Going to dinner with either or both of the Fathers was always interesting because everyone seemed to know them and to love them. During the visits the adults sat around and reminisced about when they were younger, or times when they came upstate to visit with my dad and his family.

We often took Aunt Anne to Long Island to visit with Aunt Marie and Uncle Ed. I loved those reunions. It was nice to be around our extended family. Aunt Anne loved these trips too, as she was alone in Bayonne. She and her husband Donald had a son, Donny, who died of spinal meningitis in 1945. He was just eight years old. His funeral and burial were on the day that a plane struck the Empire State Building in New York City. July twenty-eighth, 1945.

The plane, a B-25 Mitchell bomber, piloted by William Franklin Smith Jr., was attempting to land at Newark Airport in New Jersey. He became disoriented in dense fog causing him to make an incorrect turn. The plane crashed between the seventy-eighth and eightieth floors of the Empire State Building on the north side of the building.

The planes impact left a gaping hole in the north side of the building and sent one of the engines through the building and out the south side. The pilot, his two passengers and eleven others were killed.

The route to the cemetery was on the New Jersey side of the Hudson River. Across the river from the accident. I asked Aunt Anne once what that was like to see such an accident. She replied, "Honey, I never saw it". The reply was made with such overwhelming sadness. My Uncle Don, her husband, passed away in 1973.

I think my dad was a surrogate son to Aunt Anne after Donny died. Dad always seemed so protective of her. He frequently visited her after moving from Staten Island to upstate New York. When my dad was in the Army, he was stationed at Fort Dix, which is about an hour away from Bayonne. He spent his leave with Aunt Anne and Uncle Don. Dad and Aunt Anne had such affection for each other. I know Aunt Anne was my dad's favorite aunt. I was named for her.

During one of our visits to Aunt Anne's, Father Fred came to town and took us to a Mets game. We drove into the borough of Queens, New York to Shea Stadium, we kids commented and giggled about the prostitutes on the side of the road. We called the women "the ladies with the funny stockings". When Father Fred heard us laugh and giggle, he told us to pray for them. That was his nature, a kind, prayerful uncle.

We weren't scolded or reprimanded, just told to pray for them. During the game, Father Fred taught me how to keep score on the score card in the program from the game. When the game was over he signed the score card for me. It is one of my favorite treasures and I have the program to this day.

Father Andrew and Father Fred both came to visit my family when they could break away from their duties. Father Fred concelebrated all of my sibling's weddings and many of my cousin's weddings, as well. They were really busy guys. They belonged to the Missionary Servants of the Most Holy Trinity and lived in Silver Spring, Maryland.

In December, 1964, Father Fred started the Serenity Retreat League which serves members of many Twelve Step Recovery Programs. They encourage spiritual growth to help people overcome addiction. Father Fred would give more than forty retreats each year by himself. Busy as he was, he always made time for us.

Father Fred and Father Andrew made God real for me, made Jesus real for me. They were the human representation of a living God. We wrote back and forth, and their letters were always very uplifting and joy filled. I still have many of the letters. I feel so very blessed to have been able to know the people that Fathers Fred and Andrew were, and to share in their faith.

Chapter 2

I met Carmen right out of high school, we were engaged after six months of courtship. Seven months later, when I was nineteen, we eloped to Washington, D.C. When Carmen asked for my hand in marriage, my Dad told him he'd give him two hundred bucks and a ladder to take me! In the end, we got the two hundred bucks and a toaster oven!

My dad and I have always had a special bond. He joked about the ladder, but when we did elope, our marriage set my parents back a bit. I found out later that my mom went and talked to our family Priest about me and Carmen eloping. I guess she was pretty upset with me. Dad took it pretty hard as he didn't have a chance to give me away, and Carmen and I were so young. I regret that I hurt my mom and dad like that, but I was young and impetuous. If I could do it again, I don't know if I would get married like that. I probably would have waited. On the other hand, things might not have turned out the way they have. There has never been a dull moment! We have two boys, CJ and Sammy, seven years apart, that are the love of my life. I wouldn't change anything.

During my time raising the boys and our adventure years in Florida, I worked for the oldest pet business in Syracuse NY, Ebeling's Pet Center. I loved that job! It gave me the opportunity to work with animals and to teach others how to take care of new friends once they got them home. I had a veterinarian technician come into one of the stores when I was at work. She taught me how to give vaccinations and how to worm dogs and cats without killing them; a skill that really came in handy later on. I loved to learn about the animals themselves, and taking care of them.

Three years after Carmen and I married, our son CJ came along. Almost two years later, in June of 1986, I

New Leash on Life

became pregnant again. We were really excited by the news that CJ would have a sibling! However, that September, I miscarried the baby. I wrote to Father Fred, concerned because the baby was not baptized and I was destroyed by the loss. He wrote me a reply on November seventh, 1986. The following is his reply:

Dear Anne, Carmen, and Carmie, (that's what he called CJ)
 May the grace and peace of the Holy Spirit be with us forever!

Your letter was forwarded to me here at Holy Trinity where I began the second of two Serenity Retreats tonight. I hope to be back in Sterling Monday, but there will be so much catching up to do (I left Oct. 15th), your letter would be lost in the shuffle.

Needless to say, I was both surprised and happy to hear from you. I think Carmen is a "great guy" too, and Carmie is truly precious. As for my "not dancing" at (my cousin, Lisa's wedding) the wedding- I would have loved to oblige, but there are always those who are "shocked" at such carry-on by priests. Our tour guide in Hawaii did get me up on the stage to do the "Hoo-kee-lau" a few years ago.

But to get to the serious part of your letter, my dear Anne and Carmen, you didn't <u>lose</u> a <u>baby</u>. <u>You</u> <u>gained</u> a <u>saint</u>! Your child, that, with God's help you conceived, is now <u>eternally</u> <u>happy</u>, awaiting a reunion with you. You now have your own private personal intercessor before the throne of God. We all have favorite Saints: St. Theresa, St. Francis, St. Ann, St. Jude. You now have "St. Mallore"! How about that? I'm so thrilled to have another little cousin in Heaven. I'm not going to pray for him/her, but to him/her, asking him/her to ask God to make you good parents and me a better priest.

What a privilege for a boy and a girl to cooperate in the creation of a human life. Were it not for you, the baby would never know God, let alone be <u>with</u> <u>God</u>.

So dry your tears of sorrow and shed some tears of joy. God could create life without the help of humans, (Adam, for instance), but He doesn't. Since Adam it has always been a trinity: a girl, a boy, and God! How close to Divine that is. Cherish your privilege. Thank God for the power He gives you, and try again!

With kindest regards to your Mom, Dad, and family, and asking God to bless us all, I remain,

Affectionately yours,

In the Most Holy Trinity, Father Fred, S.T. (Cousin of St. Mallore!)

A most remarkable man, my cousin, Father Fred. I will keep and cherish this letter as long as I live. It brought me such hope and peace. As you can see he was a very wise man with a heart as big as an ocean. It's no wonder people loved him so.

When CJ was four, we moved to Florida. We had an adventure there, which included the birth of Sammy. The Spring of Sammy's birth year, we lost Fr. Fred. Now I have another intercessor before the throne of God! I am really sad that he is gone, and I mourn his passing, but I know what a wonderful homecoming awaited him.

That November, we moved back home to be closer to family. I went back to work at Ebeling's. We rented a small house when we moved back to Central New York from Florida. We became great friends with Nick and Bridget from across the street. We enjoyed our little house and the neighborhood but soon the time came to go house hunting and acquire something more permanent. We found a realtor, and she set us up with a list of houses to look at. Away we went!

We had looked at houses all day long. The boys were loaded in the back seat of our truck as we went to each property. We saw about a dozen houses that day. Our realtor did a good job of showing us houses, but none of them felt like home. Each house felt and looked the same to me.We didn't need anything extravagant, but I needed a home that felt special to me. So far, none had that special feel.

It was a long day. Sammy had fallen asleep in his car seat and CJ was almost asleep as well. We went to the last house on the list and decided it wasn't for us. We then stopped at an open house our realtor held in a house that we could not afford. Carmen went in and told our realtor we were done for the day. She invited us in to see this home. We were so tired. I protested because the last thing I wanted to do was look at a log home, moreover one I couldn't, as I said, afford. I walked in the front door and fell in love. I knew this would be my home.

The house had everything I had ever dreamed of in a home. It was octagonal in shape, had a separate master wing and guest wing, 2000 square feet of dream space. That is when I told Carmen "I don't care what you have to do, I want this house!" The house was built by a retired couple as their dream home. Both had been widowed, were friends from church, and decided to spend their golden years together. They had built the master suite on the opposite side of the house "for privacy from their guests", as she said.

The husband had only lived in the house a short time before he passed away and now the house was too much for his widow. She had leased the house out to a couple she had known, again, from her church, but leasing the house didn't work out. The house had been empty for about three years and needed some work.

Log homes require specific maintenance and this home had been neglected. We decided to make an offer. Our real estate agent thought we were going in too low, but what the heck, worth a shot. The house was originally listed for 144,900. After going back and forth a few times, we ended up acquiring the house for 112,000. I could not have been happier. My dream home was now my real home, such joy!

We moved in to the house on a Good Friday, a date which had significance because it was the anniversary of the former owners passing. Settling in was the easiest, most natural thing I have ever done. I was meant to be there. This house was warm and comfortable, like a great pair of jeans. It was my jeans and favorite sweater house. Just a great fit.

I loved the house. After only a few days I knew we weren't alone there. The man that built the house and had passed away was there too. He would walk around the house almost nightly, just to make sure all was well.

Our ghost was a very comforting presence. He was heard walking around as our floor boards squeaked whenever anyone walked on them. We had offers to have the noisy boards fixed, but I liked them as they were. I had never met or even seen the man until one night I saw our ghost stand in our bedroom doorway. He was a big man and a content man. I know he liked us in his home. It was palpable. You could feel positive energy in that house.

My vision of him was confirmed years later by someone that knew the man that he was indeed, a large, happy man. I didn't need to be told, I already knew!

When we bought the log cabin it was in dire need of repair, so we called a company to repair the damage caused by neglect. Carmen observed and studied what was done to our home. Along the way, he came up with different techniques in regards to cleaning the logs and application of products. Carmen enjoyed the process and decided that he could do it better, faster and neater. And he did. He decided to venture into a new occupation.

Being self-employed and building a company is very difficult. Carmen had started his log home restoration business with a few young men that he had met when he worked for another company. He had an experienced foreman that took control of the labor end.

Carmen was the salesman, sold jobs, gave estimates and did the meet and greet. He is really good at that aspect of business. Carmen has been a salesman all of his life. Then he set the employees up and they repaired and restored the homes.

The local office in Central New York soon had a great deal of work. Carmen needed help handling the phones, mail and bills. He hired a secretary. The office was very busy as his reputation got him more jobs. Carmen met a man in Colorado who was interested in opening up an office there. We had received a ton of calls from Colorado for work, so it seemed to be the right thing to do.

As Carmen was out of town a lot, I quit my job to stay home and hold down the fort. I loved the thought of being a stay at home mom and housewife. I was more than happy to oblige as I had had a really bad experience with a customer at the pet shop and was just done.

Chapter 3

Once in a while, you get someone that you just cannot please, no matter what you do. I had had a few in the past, but this one man, I won't even say gentleman, just put me over the edge. We had this young cockatiel at Ebeling's, the pet store where I worked, that was such a brat! He wouldn't cooperate at all at first.

I worked with that bird constantly until he was the sweetest thing. It took a lot of patience and time, but as with anything, you get out what you put in. He was stubborn, but I got him to trust me. He'd bite and I'd let him. I smothered him with kindness and love. He soon realized that he liked the affection more than he liked to bite me, so he relaxed. I named him Atilla, as in the Hun.

One afternoon a man came in that wanted to acquire a bird. After a discussion about what he was looking for in a bird, I introduced him to Atilla. I spent the entire afternoon with this man. I taught him about cockatiels, and in particular, Atilla. The man held Atilla and petted him. Atilla did very well with him. Afterward, I helped the man go back to his car as he needed assistance. I thought Atilla and he would be a good fit. The man came back the next day and bought Atilla, and all of his stuff. I was psyched. Atilla would have a good home.

That wasn't to be the case. A few days later I received a call at work. The man let Atilla out of his cage to walk around. The bird's wings were clipped so he looked for something to climb up on as they do not like to be down. Unfortunately, what Atilla climbed up on was a child. The child got scratched by Atilla's talons and the man went berserk. Why the man had him out in the first place, when he had company, no less, was beyond me. The bird was new to

the house and to him. Atilla hadn't even
gotten used to his new surroundings!

   The man called me, screamed that the
Atilla attacked the baby. The bird didn't
attack the child, he was trying to climb
up. When I asked him how, he told me
what had happened. I understand his
anger in that the child had been
scratched, but it was the man's fault, not
Atilla's! He really didn't want the bird,
and looked for an out. I told him I would
buy Atilla and all of his stuff back and
give him his money back. I'd keep him.
The man told me he was going to "ring
its neck and throw it against a wall"

   That's when I lost it. The store's
owner, seeing how upset I was, got on
the phone with the man and asked him
to please bring the bird back to the
store. He explained that Atilla was very
special to me and he'd refund the
money. The man replied that it was too
late, the bird was dead. The straw that
broke the camel's back. I was done. I
became a stay at home mom, which was

what I needed now. Dealing with the public can take a lot out of you. I was grateful to move on from my pet store job because I loved that bird.

Chapter 4

Carmen's business thrived. We built a great life in that house. We raised our boys there. My favorite holiday at that house was Christmas. I loved to have my Mom and Dad, Mary, Tom, and their families at our home, making memories. We'd have a huge meal, open gifts, laugh, watch "Christmas Vacation" and just have a great time. My oldest sister, Sue lives out of town, but would call during the day so as to be included in the festivities.

I was exhausted but very happy Christmas night. I sat in my living room, the fire blazed in the fireplace, content and warm, all by myself, and absorb the day. Our ghost walked by, eventually, pleased with our happy home.

The office in Colorado was busy, and the office here was busy. Carmen decided to hire a salesman as he visited jobs and gave estimates constantly.

Carmen needed to be able to visit jobs in progress and make sure every job was up to his standards. The crews were to treat every house as if it were our home, and if it wasn't, there was hell to pay. Carmen needed someone to go visit potential customers to give them an estimate and job proposal.

Carmen eventually brought another man on for an office in North Carolina to run the southeastern end of the business. Carmen worked all over the map, New England states, Colorado and its neighboring states and a lot in the south. An office in the Carolina's would be great. It would free Carmen up a bit so he could obtain more work closer to home.

Carmen traveled to North and South Carolina and Georgia. He did home shows, met homeowners and got the connections to start the office up. It was costly, but worth his time. He got a crew together and they went down to start the work. Carmen had to wait until his new manager moved down to establish the physical office.

When Carmen wasn't out of town for work, we would host Easter dinners, Halloween parties, Thanksgiving dinners, and summer parties. Our house was the place to be. When CJ played Pop Warner football and Carmen coached, we held practice in our backyard.

We striped our yard like a football field, and hooked up lights on the field. The kids had a blast. They warmed up by trying to catch our German Shepherd, Woody, around the yard. I don't know who loved the chasing more, the kids or the dog!

After practice, all of the parents would come and hang out while the kids played; we would have a big pizza party. That team was tight because the kids played well together on and off the field. The parents were happy because their kids got an amazing experience and learned how to be a team. They also learned to be respectful of their coaches, of their teammates. They learned to be fair and to play safely. Our dog, Woody, was happy being part of the team and usually ended up with a crust of pizza or two.

Woody was much more than our family pet. He was a huge part of our family. He had a big, block head, the most beautiful eyes, and a gorgeous coat. He was a sable which means that each individual hair consists of three different colors: shades of black, brown, gold and a deep red in his coat. Woody's coat changed so much over the years. We fed him a lamb and rice formula diet to keep his coat shiny and healthy. He was so soft. Most shepherds' coat becomes coarse as they grow out of their puppy coat. The fur on the ridge of his back did become more course, but his sides, face and belly were still so soft.

I loved his ears. They never changed. They were like satin. So, so soft. He loved to be loved. Some dogs put up with it, but he loved to be loved. I obliged. There is nothing like the unconditional love of a dog. You can feel terrible, have the most awful day, then you come home to a dog that believes the sun rises and sets because of you. There is no feeling as great as that love. Blessed is the person that owns a dog. He is graced with a never-ending love.

Such an amazing relationship. My brother Tom always said I had the weirdest animals. My animals always seem to behave out of the norm for most animals. This is definitely true for Woody and our Princess Kitty. Woody loved Princess. Princess loved Woody. I bought him a cow femur for Christmas one year. Woody really enjoyed that bone. So did Princess. She would be on one end of that thing gnawing away and he'd be on the other.

I don't think they knew that they were supposed to be arch enemies. It was an amazing relationship. They would chase each other around the house until exhausted. Princess knew that Woody wasn't allowed on the kitchen floor and she took full advantage of that. The kitchen was her "free" space. She knew Woody wouldn't chase her there.

Princess always found the sunniest spot on the living room floor to take a bath and clean herself. Woody would go over and plop himself down next to her and she'd give him a bath too. He would let her clean his face and ears and the two of them would fall asleep in the sunbeam on the floor. Happy, safe and warm in each other's embrace

Woody was my shadow. I would trip over him all the time. He was a big baby and a huge momma's boy. I love to work in my garden, and as I weeded, Woody would be next me with all of the weeds I had put beside me in a pile, on top of him. I hadn't realized he was so close to me, and as I pulled weeds, I unknowingly threw them on top of him. He didn't care. He helped and that is all that mattered.

Such a brilliant dog. Woody would take off running after his girlfriend Goldie, from next door, full out gallop, but when we snapped our fingers, he would be at our side in an instant. He knew that when I came in from grocery shopping he was to go wait in his kennel until I called him.

Same thing with dinner. I just had to take a plate out of the cupboard and Woody knew he was not allowed to beg at the table. Down to his crate he would go, again, until we called him. His crate was never used as punishment. Dogs are by nature a denning animal. This was his den. His space to go when he wanted some privacy or a nap. He slept in his crate at night. It was his haven.

Everyone that met Woody, loved him. He had such a gentle soul. He was great with kids. When Sammy was little, we would have him run to the edge of our backyard. We held Woody until Sam got to the property line. Woody would then be released to go "get Sammy". Woody would run out to where Sammy was and bring him back by circling around and around Sammy until he was back to us. For doing such a great job, Woody got tons of hugs, kisses and praise.

He adored our little neighbor, Morgan too. Morgan would come over for our daily visit and she and Woody would chase each other around our dining room table. Morgan could lay on the floor with a treat and Woody would lay next to her and let her play with it before gently taking in from her when offered. He would play for hours in a pile of leaves with Cj, Sammy, and Morgan's brother AJ. Woody would join in any game the kids played and was so gentle and careful with them all.

Carmen and I took CJ and Sammy to the Outer Banks for Thanksgiving and left Woody at a conventional kennel. When we got back, he was miserable. Thin and dehydrated, I felt horrible that we had gone, had a good time and my beloved had only been let out twice a day. No one stayed there at night or on weekends. They had someone come in to let their boarders out twice a day on weekends, but that was all.

Woody was a baby and wanted to be talked to and hugged. Never again would we leave our beloved dog at a kennel.

The next time we went away, we left Woody home with one of the neighbors to watch him and let him out. Being Woody, he was outside playing and found another neighbors compost pile. He ate a pineapple rind out of the compost. It happened on the day we got home. He hacked the rind back up and seemed fine until a few months later. Woody had developed an enlarged esophagus.

We took him to the vet and they ran tests on him. We were told that he could have surgery to try to repair the esophagus, but the chances were only 50/50 that it would help. He came out of the anesthesia he was given for the tests very badly. I don't think he could survive that again. We got a second opinion and we were told that at 10 years old, chances were not good for a favorable outcome. We were all devastated.

The point in time arrived when Woody couldn't keep his food down. I bought him canned food and spoon fed him and massaged his throat to make it go past a pocket that caught the food. Shortly after, he couldn't keep water down and we knew it was time. This magnificent 120 pound dog was wasting away. I couldn't let that happen. He had given us all he had in his 10 years, the best we could give him now was peace.

We called our vet and took Woody on his last ride. Sammy stayed with AJ and Morgan and their mom and dad, Linda and Alex from next door. Carmen, CJ and I took Woody into the vet's office. CJ made it as far as the waiting room, but had to go back outside as he sobbed.

Carmen and I took Woody in the room and that is when he decided that he felt better and acted as if nothing was wrong! At the house before we left, he was dying and now he was himself again. Maybe he knew he was going to be at peace soon.

Carmen left the room, he couldn't handle the emotion. He realized he had left me there alone to deal with this, then he came back in. We got Woody up on the table and Woody was given the "youth shot" as we call it.

I held Woody's beautiful face in my hands, thanked him, kissed him, loved him, kissed him more and then let him go. His eyes locked in mine forever. I tried not to cry because I didn't want to upset him, but I couldn't stop. He knew, he knew, how very special he was. He knew how much we all loved him.

At home without my Woody was horrible. I went in, became very angry, and just cried. I laid in bed and punched the pillows, got up and went outside to my swing where Woody and I always sat to watch the day, and sobbed. I second guessed my decision. Should we have tried something else? Could we have done more? Should we have gone through with the surgery?

What it boiled down to was that I didn't want him to suffer. The anesthesia alone might have killed him in his weakened state. I know we did the right thing but I felt like shit.

For two weeks, I didn't want to get out of bed. Mourning a person is so hard, but I honestly think that mourning a dog that loved you with all of his heart, without judgment, without looking for a return, is just as hard. A broken heart is a broken heart either way. The doorbell would ring, I waited for Woody to bark. When Goldie was out, I looked for Woody. So did Goldie. At bed time he always gave Princess Kitty and Jackie the rabbit a kiss goodnight before getting in his crate. They waited. Life became very different.

Princess went into mourning for a year. Jackie, our rabbit, passed the following spring. Amazingly, life did go on. We called the breeder that we had gotten Woody from to tell him of his passing. He let us know that one of Woody's nieces had had a litter of pups. There was one sable male in the litter. We knew we couldn't replace what we had with Woody, but we could honor his memory and fill the void by getting another puppy. Into our lives came Wiley.

I wish I had a nickel for every time Carmen commented on Wiley's intelligence or lack of. He really wasn't. Wiley was a puppy that had the enormous task of filling huge paw prints! Woody, after all, was brilliant! This puppy, not so much.

Wiley was stubborn, that's all. It took us so much longer to teach him things. Woody would come when you snapped your fingers. Wiley thought it was a game. He also got away with a lot more because I trained him as opposed to Carmen's more strict ways. I'm the Momma, even to the dog.

Woody could be anywhere off leash and he'd always come back. With Wiley, um, no. He had to be on a leash or he'd take off after a butterfly. He was all about fun and playing. Woody knew there was a time and place for that and he wanted to please us. Woody liked to work, Wiley likes to play. They are so different in so many ways, but in the affection department, both are the most lovable, gentle dogs.

I know now that Woody wouldn't put up with the antics that go on at Wags where dogs jump and play all the time. He was much too serious for all of this nonsense! He was a German Shepherd after all! Proud, regal, not like the silly dog Wiley! I am so glad they are so different. There can only be one Woody and one Wiley and I am just fine with that.

Chapter 5

At one point, Carmen went to buy product for our log home company, and was told by his secretary that there wasn't enough in the account to cover it. How could that possibly be? He had been working his butt off! Carmen's answer was to go out and work harder to make more money. He knew the company was busy, knew he made good money...

Then he received a call from a customer in Colorado who complained that they hadn't seen any of his employees in a month, or the manager either, yet, we sent pay checks. Carmen took our guys from here, to Colorado, to finish the job and closed the office. After an audit we found that personal bills were being paid out of our account including car loans, cell phones, mortgage, and utilities. Carmen's company was paying for the manager's lifestyle. This makes my

stomach hurt. He could write a book
about what not to do in business!!
Chapter one, Trust no one!

Chapter 6

Sundays during football season were full of games. My brother Tom and his two boys, Tommy and Chris would come over for whatever games were on TV. I built a big fire in our fireplace, and we had snacks and drinks during the games. Later on, I would make dinner for us all. Tom's wife Lisa teaches figure skating and she taught all day, but would come to our house later in the evening. Our kids watched the games, went outside, or played in the basement. Sundays were good.

Lisa and I were best friends as kids. We lived in the same neighborhood, a few blocks apart. She dated my brother Tom in high school and I was glad when they got married! She felt like a sister to me, so it's nice she and Tom got together. When Lisa was pregnant for Tommy we sat and talked about the things we did as kids and hoped the boys didn't do them!

We knew that our children would grow up to be the best of friends and make great memories of their own. We are so fortunate that our talks came to fruition. CJ, Sammy, Tommy and Chris are so close. Their core group of friends are each other. The boys are also very close with my sister Mary's girls, Elizabeth and Lauren. The boys are very protective of those girls. I feel kinda bad for a boy that likes one of my nieces. Any potential suitor will have four male cousins to go through first!

Carmen and Tom really enjoy watching football together. We are New York Giant's fans and in Tom's house, it's the New York Jets all the way. There is a rivalry that exists, to say the least. Carmen, Tom and our boys have been to a few preseason professional football games and had so much fun! One year, Lisa and I joined the boys in our RV for a game. Lisa and I watched the game in the RV while the boys were in the Giant's stadium. A great experience. I'm not sure who had the better time.   The boys went a few more times for a "man's date". They always came back with great stories! Carmen and Tom are both a little twisted. I often say that Carmen married me because of my brother

In the summertime, we had the pool, cookouts and our annual summer party, with a band and lots of friends, music, food, and beer! Carmen and I have friends that play in a two separate Syracuse based bands, The Rhythm Method and The Horn Dogs, but for our party, they played together.   They made our parties!   Neighbors that didn't come to the party would sit in their lawns and listen to the bands. After the party, Jim, John and Jodi from the Rhythm Method, Carmen, myself and a few other friends cooked hot dogs and hamburgers on the grill, laughed and sang into the wee hours of the morning. We had to close the garage door, as to not wake the neighborhood!

Chapter 7

When the time came for the manager to go and open the office in North Carolina, he decided that he'd rather work from central New York. The whole idea for an office in the Carolinas was so that Carmen would have an office in the southeast, to handle the southeast! He spent a lot of money for the start-up. A new office didn't happen as we could no longer get a hold of the manager. Carmen ended up traveling back and forth to get the jobs he had set up for the so called manager, completed. Ugh.

The salesman we had hired to relieve some of Carmen's work load, made commission on the sale of a job and was drastically underbidding the jobs. It didn't matter to him, evidently, that he bid the job too low, he still got paid. By the time the job was done and the job costing analysis was done, we were losing money. A lot of money. To add insult to injury, when we hired this salesman, as an incentive, we agreed to work on his cabin for free. He sued us to fulfill that contract after we let him go. Such a gem. We worked harder to pay our bills.

Chapter 8

Our house was the Friday night party spot with a lot of friends and family. We built a bar in our basement and it was always full on a Friday night. Our bar was the place to be. I had my drums in the basement and could easily be persuaded to play along with the music.

I don't consider myself a great or even good drummer, but I have tons of fun. Jokes and laughs were in abundance in our basement bar. Our stomachs would hurt from laughing. Life was good. I used to say that when I died and got to the pearly gates, and God asked me what I did with the wonderful gift of life He had given me; I would reply that I had a hell of a time!

I began to miss work. Being home was great, but I missed working in the pet industry. I had loved the animals and the teacher aspect of my job. Our boys were getting older and I wanted something to do. I loved being a stay at home mom, but I enjoyed working too. After Woody died, Carmen and I discussed building a dog wash and kennel. A place that was better than what was out there. I didn't want anyone's beloved to be "stored" as Woody had been. We could do better than what we had experienced.

Carmen had a friend, Dick that had a building that he stored cars in. Carmen approached Dick with our idea of constructing a pet motel inside of his building. He laughed, but knew that we were determined and had a good idea. Our kennel had to be unique. It had to be more like home, more comfortable for our guests. Carmen decided our business should be called Wags. Why? Because it is catchy. On many occasions, especially Friday nights at our bar, we discussed exactly what we wanted to do in terms of a business concept.

Chapter 9

Not long after the call from Colorado and the mess with the Southeastern office, our lives began to spiral out of control. We left a crew in North Carolina to do a job and one of the employees took one of our company trucks and went to Texas to see friends, per diem and all. His foreman didn't think it necessary to tell us as he and the others did the work. This was a paid vacation on us, without approval, of course.

Bills that we thought were getting paid, were not. Work that we paid employees to do, we had to do ourselves. We were cruising along at the home office after Carmen let the salesman go, but it wasn't enough. We fell farther and farther behind financially.

It would be one thing if we just took and blew the money we made, but we didn't and we weren't. I know that is what some people think. Those people don't know how hard we worked. What Carmen and I had when he started the company, we owned. We borrowed to keep up with our growth. We grew too fast, trusted too many people, surrounded ourselves with the wrong people and as a result, came back to bite us.

The Colorado operation, done, Southern branch, done. Managers, salesman and secretary, all gone. Now it was just myself, Carmen and one of the remaining guys we trusted, working jobs together to survive. We busted our butts trying to get jobs done. It wasn't enough to save us. As Carmen says, bailing us out was like trying to bail out the Titanic with a coffee cup.

We filed Chapter 13 bankruptcy to protect our home and to reorganize our debts so that we could pay them. We hired an attorney, Bill, who told us he would help us keep our home. We were then assigned a trustee to whom we would send our payments. The trustee in turn would disperse the payments amongst our creditors.

Carmen and I would be able to keep our home. Things would be tight, but we'd be able to stay in our home. Dick agreed to lease out half of his building to us to build the new pet business. Carmen and I worked the log home business and also sold off personal items to pay our debts.

We made our trustee payments and also our mortgage payments. We were going to be all right. That was until September of 2006. We received our check back from the mortgage company along with a letter stating that our lawyer had not filed a certain order to protect our house. The mortgage company would be selling our home. The letter arrived three days after our house was sold.

Carmen and I were called into Bill's, office and informed by him that he had "dropped the ball". In moving to a new law firm, neither Bill nor his assistant had filed the protection order regarding our home and the bankruptcy. The protection order had "slipped through the cracks". We were out. We no longer owned our home.

The bank took our home and sold it, no auction, sold. Bill attempted to fight the bank over the course of the next several months to reverse the sale, but the deal was done and we were out. We were advised by a friend, who is also an attorney, that we could sue Bill. It wouldn't get us our house back and to be quite honest, I could not go thru the anguish of that again.

My heart was broken. It was a death and I went thru all of the stages of grief, shock and denial, pain and sadness, bargaining, rage, depression and then anxiety. The last stage is acceptance, but I wasn't ready for that yet.

Carmen and I had started work on Wags, but we weren't even close to opening and now we had to be out of our home. Where would we stay?? We had offers from my parents, Tom and Lisa and our friends, Bridget and Nick to stay with them. We declined their offers, generous as they were. This was our problem, not theirs. We had to take care of us. Bill took our Chapter 13 and turned it into a 7 which we didn't like, but had no choice. We had nothing left.

Dick agreed to lease out half of his building to us. Without so much as a blueprint, but with this idea in Carmen's head, we started to build Wags. Carmen sketched out a drawing on paper to present to the town board, but that was it. The layout and design was in his head. Carmen and I started cleaning up the building in November of 2006.

The first thing that had to be done was to remove all of Dick's cars. We would lease only half of the building. That is 2500 feet of clean up. No worries, I love to clean. Cleaning is like therapy to me. Stress me out and you will get a clean house. My mom's storage cabinet was one of my targets. That thing was always in disarray. Something would set me off and I would clean and straighten the whole cabinet!

I have no problem cleaning and reorganizing things. The building would be a breeze. The cars were removed so I started washing floors and getting stuff organized. The building was rather new, so it wasn't in too bad of shape. There were a few stains on the floor from the cars, some cob webs and dust, nothing major.

By Christmas, we had most of the building cleaned up. Thank God for my faith. Christmas is not about gifts and such, but about time together with my boys. We couldn't afford gifts, but at least we had dinner and a tree. We came into the New Year with the hope that somehow we would get our house back. We still lived in the house as Bill went after the mortgage company for not giving us enough notice when our house went up for sale. We'll see how that goes...

Somehow each day came and went. I just went with each day as if it were the last day, with no concept of time. We packed up what we had left in our home and brought our stuff to the shop. In the early morning hours of May 1st, 2007, we left our home for the last time and moved into a hotel in Camillus, NY where we stayed for a week with Princess Kitty and Wiley. After that, we stayed at what would become Wags. We were homeless, but not really because we had each other.

Chapter 10

We are pretty lucky that not all of our friends bailed. Jim and John from the band that used to play at our house, along with their girlfriends, Virginia and Barb, came in to help with the construction of Wags. Carmen has no real written blueprints, but knows what he wants to build. I don't know that giving a tool to John is such a good idea as he picked up the nail gun and quicker than we could tell him not to touch the trigger, a nail sailed through the building! I think we are working with the Three Stooges!

June, a women we met through the band, and who has become one of my dearest friends, has been amazing. She helped with the building while her husband Rob is at work. She and Rob bought most of our furniture from the house. It's hard to go to her house and see my living room and dining room there, but I'm so grateful for them buying it as the proceeds enabled us to buy building material. Now June is helping to assemble those same building materials into Wags.

These are my "silver friends". There was a song I learned when in Girl Scouts called "Make new friends". It went "Make new friends, but keep the old. One is silver and the other, gold"[1]. We'd sing the song in a round and I never forgot it. My silver friends I've had for a while, but are 'new-ish'. My gold friends I've had most of my life. What happened to us didn't really affect the gold friends as I don't see them so much anymore, but when we do get together, it's like we were together yesterday.

"The disappeared" are the friends that for one reason or another left when the good times faded. My silver friends are coming through, I don't know if that is good or bad after the nail incident, but I

---

[1] Author unknown "Make New Friends" Girl Scout Song Book

appreciate them none the less. We had started the construction before we left the house so by the time we actually had to get out, some of the shell was already up. The skeleton was in place.

We set up what would be home at, what I call now, the shop. After we left the motel, we went and bought a tent to set up inside the shop. We put in an inflatable mattress for us to sleep on. We put the mattress from Sammy's bed in there for him to sleep on. Princess Kitty and Wiley both sleep in the tent with us.

With no cell service, no cable and no TV in the building, we are left to talk before going to sleep. It's nice. Like camping. Sort of. We go to Mom and Dad's house and shower at night. In the morning we use the bathroom in the shop to wash up, brush our teeth and get ready for the day. We take Sammy to school and Carmen and I build or run errands to get materials.

Usually, we skip lunch and either eat something microwaved or a lot of nights

Tom and Lisa have us at their house for a cookout. We have no stove, no oven, and no shower. There is a 2 gallon water heater. I think its 2 gallon, it's not much, but we make due. We do have the microwave, and our grill eventually found its way here. In the mornings I disassemble the tent and we get to work. It's not living, it's surviving, getting by, and it is hard. I cry every day, I want to go home, I know I can't and it's killing me.

So, with that being said, some of the words that follow are from my journal I kept. I was pretty irrational in those first months as I look back and read my writings. Anger was a huge part of my daily life. Depression never left even though I was put on antidepressants. I wanted people to be as miserable as I was, given my disarray at the loss of my house, worry over our future and day to day living.

You will see that my journal entries are my raw emotions to the places, times and events that occurred during the course of my journey. I wrote from the core of my essence and given that fact, I choose not to edit, adapt or modify some of my writings. This is important because you see my road from darkness to light and my hope is that you are inspired along the way. I was in an imperfect state of mind when I penned this. I need to keep it perfectly imperfect.

I also did not date some of my entries. Some days, I just wrote. Dates didn't seem all that important to me at the time. Important dates, I wrote down. Times I really needed to remember. When you go through a life changing experience like this, time seems to stand still to wait for you to catch up and process what is happening. Maybe it's a survival mechanism to keep you from going totally insane. Maybe it helps us cope.

Chapter 11

May 6th, 2007

Carmen bought me this journal today.
I guess to save my life. I need to write
again, to put into words what I'm feeling.
I need to get things out of me and gone.
First, let me say, that it is another
beautiful day. Sunny, breezy and warm.
It's a lot cooler in the shade. Sam is at
the desk doing homework. Carmen went
to see a friend about using his trailer to
get the lawn mower here so we can clean
up this yard.

My handwriting is pretty sloppy. My
wrist doesn't work quite the same
anymore since the accident Feb 16th. We
were coming home from plowing, trying
to make some extra money, when we
were forced off the road by a woman in a
Saturn, in our lane, on a country road in
Camillus, NY. It was either hit her head
on and then hit the truck behind her or,
take the ditch. We took the ditch.

Neither she nor the truck behind her stopped to help us even though our truck was on its side, in the ditch. I could only see about an inch out of my window and Carmen was hanging by his seatbelt over me. I smacked my right arm and wrist pretty good against the door. Carmen wrenched his lower back. The truck is fine. Talk about a run of bad luck! I have a cold spot on my palm between my ring finger and pinky, weird. It hurts to write, but I have to. It's not a want, but a need.

My house is gone. How does it go with mourning? Sadness, anger, disbelief, bargaining, acceptance? I'm angry. We found out Friday that they are asking 189,900 for our house. We cannot afford that. Our former life is gone, done, over, and I can't seem to get over it. This is a deep physical pain. An ache. An anxiety that I have never felt before.

I want to hole up in the house with a gun. In my living room. I want to sit on the hearth of my fireplace and make the cops come and kill me. Then I could stay. I'd be in my house always. I wouldn't have to leave. I wouldn't hurt any of the officers, but force them to kill me. I think about that all the time. And, I'm not afraid. I don't feel anything about it.

I want Bill to know just what he did to me by "dropping the ball". I want the mortgage company to know. Then, I know that they wouldn't care and the only one it would hurt is my family. Sometimes, I don't even care about that. Then I think I'm awful. I'm too rational to do something like that. I get scared that Carmen's going to hate me for crying all the time. No one wants to be around someone who is sad all the time.

I don't like being around others, I get very stressed out when we go see anyone. I feel very anti- social. I have anxiety attacks at night. It's like being startled but it's not short or quick, but lasts a long time. I can't catch my breath and my heart starts to race. I get sweaty and terrified.

I get separation anxiety when Carmen is not here. I'm a bit freaked right now because he's been gone what seems like hours, but has probably been only an hour. I try to stay upbeat for Sammy and for Carmen. I was always the optimist here. Now, Carmen is the optimistic one.

I don't trust my gut anymore. I used to know things, absolutely, no doubt, know things. Now, I feel like I'm flying blind. I can count on nothing. I don't trust anyone anymore. I want to, but I can't. I don't want, to want, to help anyone, but I can't help still wanting to save the world! Why? Why? I need to focus on us, no one else.

I keep feeling that, Oh my God if this happened to one of our friends, no question, they would be at my house, no question! There would be Wegman's gift certificates or dinner or something! We were always there for our friends whenever they needed something, it didn't matter what it was. I didn't expect anything in return but that's exactly what we are getting. Man that sucks.

I feel like we have a cold that people are afraid to catch! You are supposed to be there for your friends, we always were, yet, nothing. The friend Carmen went to see about using his trailer, said no. Carmen never denied him anything. Another friend, Kevin, he brought his trailer here. So, Kevin, the friend that never asked for a thing, never was in need, pulled through for us. The one that asked for favors and were given them, denied us. Interesting.

Carmen went and got the mower, but not my grill. He said a couple was looking at our house. Carmen told them what happened to us, they said they wouldn't buy it. He then proceeded to tell them that no, it's a great home, a great place to raise a family and we were happy there. Just needs a lot of work.

I hate the realtor that is listing our house as this is his niche, selling homes that have been foreclosed upon. I hate Bill for dropping the ball, I hate the stupid mortgage company, and banks in general!!! I want to go home, I want to go home. I just want to go home!

I am homesick, then I look at Sammy and Carmen, and with them, I am home. I feel so bad for Terry. She knows what it feels like to lose home. Her husband Ken was her home and now, he's dead. Carmen met Terry when she hired him to do work on her log home located west of St. Louis, Missouri. They became fast friends. Over the course of the next years, they would talk regularly as she too is a big football fan. Only problem is she is a Ram's fan. The rivalry between them was lighthearted and fun and I couldn't wait to meet her.

Carmen was at Terry's house when the terror of 9/11 happened. It was so hard having him that far away on such an awful day. We spent a lot of time on the phone during all of that. I was so afraid, as we all were. He was so far away.

We had tickets for a Giant's game against the Rams in 2003. Carmen called Terry and asked if she wanted to go. Of course she did! At the time, she was dealing with a messy divorce, and she asked her son Scott to join her. I had never met Terry until Carmen brought them home from the airport. No worries, I loved her immediately! It was as if I'd known her all my life.

Terry and Carmen picked on each other like a brother and sister would, it was so much fun! We went to the game, Giants won of course, and it was a great trip! Terry got through her divorce and met a wonderful man named Ken. They met at a Rams game, go figure. He adored her and she him.

Terry brought Ken here in the summer of 2005 so we could meet him. Carmen had to be sure Ken was honorable as Terry was his "big sister". He took him for a ride in his Mustang, got it up to about 100 miles per hour. He then asked Ken what his intentions were regarding Terry. I don't quite know the response, but Terry and Ken were married in 2006. During their time here, we went to another Giants, Rams game. Again, the Giants won. Ken had to wear Carmen's Giants jersey the rest of the day!

We took Terry and Ken on a day trip to Cooperstown as they had never been. What a great trip that was! We stayed up late every night of their visit talking and just having the best time. We got to see their wedding via the internet in September, 2006. Ken would call Carmen just to catch up and discuss what was going on in the world. Carmen loved those calls. Terry and I would inevitably add our two cents and we'd laugh over the phone!

Ken and Terry had built a home on a lake together outside of St. Louis and were so happy. Terry had her Prince Charming. On his way home from work in November of 2006, Ken suffered a massive heart attack while driving, and crashed into an off ramp traffic divider. He was dead instantly. Terry called to tell us. Hearing this news was awful.

This lovely man, this sweet man, gone. We were devastated, all of us, we cared so much for him. Carmen talked to her daily. Terry was beside herself. Because we were struggling financially at that time, we were unable to be with Terry during this terrible time. Thankfully, she has a lot of friends nearby to surround her. I would just die, no joke, just die. More of my life has been with Carmen than without him. Right now, he is who I am. How do you live without that?

Chapter 12

I've decided I hate morning. I don't want to get up. Actually I don't want to wake up. It's better when I'm asleep. No worries or problems. It's all good. Man, my hand and arm are really bothering me today. Last night too. I took ibuprophin this morning. Sam didn't go to school because he didn't finish a paper. This has to stop. We need to get normalcy back for him. This sucks.

Carmen wants to go to see Bill today. I'm afraid to go see him. I don't want to say something bad or be intimidated by him. I can't handle it. At dinner last night, I just wanted to run. It was great, but there was too much stress. I pray all the time, still. I guess the only faith that I have lost is with myself. I can't seem to decide anything anymore. I used to do things like get dressed without even thinking. Not anymore. It's like I have to analyze, second guess everything that I do.

So, we went and saw Bill. Not so good. I did not want to go, but Carmen made me. I don't know what Carmen was looking for. Maybe for this all to be a big misunderstanding. Bill apologized to us for losing the house again, but then defended himself by saying that we couldn't afford the house anyway. Well, we were affording it 'til he screwed up! Bill also said that if we didn't sue him that his fees would be dropped! Great! Kind of you! We left.

About fifteen minutes later Bill called and again said he had done all he could, and that we couldn't have afforded to stay in our home. Bill said he's going to send us a recap letter and asked for our address. Where? At the motel we are staying at???

What he will probably do is send us an astronomical final bill and tell us how lucky we are that we don't have to pay it. Can't wait for that mail. Needless to

say, I did not sleep last night. I
watched our room get lighter and got
madder and madder, sadder and sadder.
If it happens again tomorrow morning
I'm gonna take another anti-depressant.
Just hate that.

Our friends, Meg and Ed took us to
dinner last night. Their daughter, Alicia
is Sammy's girlfriend. We met when our
kids started to date. We went to Tully's
where the service and company were
really good. It was nice to get out for a
bit and get my mind on something else.
We went back to Wags and tried to hook
up the internet to no avail, so we headed
back to the motel.

Coming back to the motel from the
shop, I couldn't figure out where we
were going as we made a turn where we
would normally go straight to go home.
I had a bit of an anxiety attack, so I
grabbed Carmen's hand. I was terrified!
I want to go home. Carmen and I went
by our house today and people were
there, at my house, cleaning it out! All I

can think is that I want everyone that is involved in this to be on our side of it and see what it's like to have this happen to them. In reality, I wish this experience on no one. It's just too horrible.

Carmen and Sammy have been working on the upstairs area. We are going to make that our apartment. Every morning I have to take down the tent and box it up in case anyone from the town comes in. We aren't supposed to stay here but we don't have a choice. The boys are going to put the water heater in the utility room and the shower upstairs, between the two bedrooms. It looks pretty good up there and will give us some privacy as well.

We went shopping today to pick up a water heater and a shower insert. The water heater is expensive. I wished for a miracle as our budget is so small. We have to be out of the hotel tomorrow morning as they are booked up due to

Syracuse University's graduation weekend.

It's hot out again today. When I hooked up the thermometer at the shop yesterday it registered 87.4 degrees. Yup, it was warm. Not bad in the shop as it faces north. Wiley is doing better. He's eating better and seems better. He seems to be adjusting well. I don't remember what I wrote previously, so I may repeat myself sometimes.

CJ stopped and picked up the air conditioner last night and said the death mobile is gone from the house. We should report it stolen, press charges. If I was home, I'd be opening up the pool today... I'm not home.

So, we've been busy. We moved out of the hotel on Thursday morning. The owners wanted us to take a different room, but it was time to go. We packed everything up and moved out. We are now staying at Wags. Carmen wanted a screened tent to sleep in, but we bought a camping tent for forty-nine dollars, and it's better and cheaper.

Sam stayed with Tom and Lisa Thursday night. Friday was very eventful. The codes enforcement officer called and told us to go ahead and build that our plan went through with the board. We found out the price of the house was dropped to 144,900. We offered 145,800 a few months ago, and they refused, so why this now?

Bill gave us the name of a friend of his that might want to help us buy back our house, so we went and talked to him. On the way to his house we discussed what we should do. He did indeed offer us the money to buy the house, but we turned him down. It was a great meeting. He told us we would bounce back and said we must really love each other to survive this. Yup, true. He said if we found something we could afford, that he'd help us out. Cool.

We are calling tomorrow about the house next door to my parents. The house has been empty for a few months. It would be great if we could get it cheap and would help out Mom and Dad. I was at their house today again to shower, as we don't have one at Wags, and it was great. My dad is coming to Wags in the morning to give us a hand. We have the utility room partly closed in with new flooring. Looks great.

Mom and Dad's 50th Anniversary party was Sunday. A good day. A pretty good weekend, in fact. I took Lisa to pick up Tommy in Oswego on Friday. We brought all of his stuff back in our truck. I had a little panic attack when we got there, but I don't think they noticed. I got it under control pretty quickly. Saturday I helped Lisa to plant flowers in the little pots she decorated for the tables at the anniversary party. They are so beautiful. We went to Mass on Sunday. There was a Baptism and they had Mom and Dad renew their vows. I cried.

After Mass, Sue, Mary, Lisa and I went to the fire house and decorated. The guests started showing up and the day went by so fast. The party was from 3-7. We ate at 5 and a lot of people left right after. It was a great party and everyone had a good time. We all stayed and cleaned up and then Carmen, Sammy and I came back "home".

Monday, Tuesday, and today, not so good. I had another nightmare last night. Carmen woke me up from it. I was crying in my sleep. I just want this awful dream to be over, to be back where we were before all of this.

I get, and got asked so many times about the house. It's a knife in my heart, a real, physical pain. I can't take it sometimes. I can't think about the house because I get a blinding rage and want to hit something. I want to scream and rip something apart. I wonder how Bill would feel if he had no home to go to at the end of the day? If he had to sleep in a tent at night and have people look down on him. How would he deal with it? No, he goes home to his lovely home with his family, no worries.

We're here, no shower. No real bed. No home and I am so homesick! I just want to go home! Can anyone hear me???? I want this to be a bad dream that I will NOW wake up out of. I'm terrified of our future. I don't trust my gut any longer. I don't pray for anything but the health and welfare of my family. I ask God for nothing because I'm afraid. Afraid, I guess, to ask. I think he's mad at me anyway. I don't want to bother Him with my trivial stuff. I'm just going to have to give it all to Him and see what He does with it and just accept the results. What else can I do? I can't control what happens, so why try?

I used to think I was special. No more. I'm just like everyone else. I don't trust my intuition anymore. My intuition lied to me and let me down. I feel like I'm drowning. I don't want to bring my boys down. I love them so much and don't want to hurt them in any way, so I try to be strong. I don't want to get mean. I don't want to lose my relationship with my sons. I need to get better, happy, whatever, but I feel like I'm drowning.

I don't think the meds work as well as they used to. The thought of killing myself and being rid of this pain is a daily thing. Not just once a day or a fleeting thought. I miss Morgan (the little girl that lived next door) so much, but I don't know if I could handle seeing her. I miss her mom, and all the great times we had together. I miss her family and the friendship we shared. I'm not angry, but my heart hurts.

Each person handles situations in different ways. In our case, some of our friends distanced themselves because they couldn't handle what happened to us. It was inconceivable to them that their friends, with whom they had spent many, many great times with, were suddenly not those people anymore.

Unable to deal with the loss we were experiencing, they backed away.

Other friends left because we didn't have the means to party the way we used to. We weren't able to host the big party anymore or to buy a friend a drink at the bar or for that matter, go to a bar. It isn't the case with all of our friends, but some. It's too bad because I am grateful for all of my friendships. I can't regret any of my friendships because I have learned something from each one, especially the ones where they really needed a friend, or a favor, or a break. You learn a lot from someone in need.

May 28th, 2007

Sammy stayed at Alicia's last night. I don't know why we allowed that! What was I thinking? I was thinking that I trust them and he needed to get away from work for a while. Plus, her parents, Meg and Ed, are there too. No worries.

My left knee is blown up. It feels like, when I walk, that my kneecap is pushed into whatever is there. Man, it hurts. My right knee is my bad one! I don't get this. My handwriting is awful because my hand is numb but achy. I feel like something is, no, something is, stopping them from a full bend. Must be the swelling. My left knee doesn't even look like mine.

Carmen is cleaning out the other side of the building. The RV that was over there was taken out yesterday. We had a cookout here yesterday too. Nick and Bridget, stopped by to see if we wanted to meet up later. They have remained a constant in our lives, even offering up their home when we had to leave ours. I would have enjoyed going out, but my head, neck and knees are killing me so we didn't go. I want to wake up from this nightmare. This is so wrong. This is not the way our life was going.

Mom called and I had to go up the ladder to get the phone. We don't have stairs to the second floor yet. Up, not so bad. Down, bad! It hurts up into my hip. Sciatic nerve maybe. I took one ibuprophin. It's not working. I would take another but I don't want to get up again.

I'm sitting in the sun, on my bench in the yard with my feet up. Lovely. It is Memorial Day weekend. Carmen had to physically get me down the ladder this morning and walk me to the bathroom. I could not do it on my own. The back of my head down into my neck hurts. Everything hurts.

Haven't seen much of CJ lately. I understand. He has his job, his own place, his girlfriend. He has a life of his own. He's young and constantly busy. And I miss him. I think he is handling all of this mess by staying away. I don't blame him. We have to get this place up and running. We need to make cash and everyday we're not open, we lose money. We are going to Meg and Ed's for a cookout. That will be nice.

Carmen saw one of the women we used to be friends with in the grocery store. He said hello, but she just looked at him. Looked thru him. How sad. A neighbor of ours put a cash, as is, offer on the house. The offer was turned down. The offer that was accepted was for three thousand dollars less and contingent on an inspection. And, they have to get a mortgage. How weird is that? I wished for a guardian angel to just get our house back for us. Wishful thinking.

I can't believe I'm living in a tent, in a storage building and a few short years ago, my life was great. Next chapter??? Carmen says this is the beginning of great things for us, but as I sit here now, looking at our situation, I'm not so sure. I don't trust my gut. I say that a lot, I know, but my gut had never failed me before.

I try not to ask God for anything because I don't want to bother Him. I don't know why He is angry with me. Maybe He's not. He has more to do than take care of me. I know that's true. I'm not the only one on this earth that needs help. I'm simply not that important.

Why can't bad things happen to me? Where do you go, what do you do when you lose hope? You die. Maybe I already did die and this is hell. I don't know how it could be because it's so beautiful today, but maybe it's all just a cruel joke. Maybe we just go on and on and on without even knowing when one life starts and when one ends. I'm 45 and I feel like I'm falling apart.

When you wish for death you think it will be easy and painless yet, that's not always the case. Look at Uncle Ted. He held on so long and suffered so much. Why? Doesn't make sense, all of that suffering. I think about death and dying a lot. Then my parents stop by or call. No such thing as coincidence. I got the best hug from my Dad. He and Mom stopped in after shopping for a picnic table. I really needed a good Daddy hug today, and there he was. Just when I needed him.

Man, it is beautiful out. Warming up. Lighter winds. Summery, puffy clouds, nice. CJ got me a bird feeder for Mother's Day. I have "the regulars" that stop by. Our motel is extended outdoors by the dining area for birds. I just need bird houses now!

We went to Meg and Ed's for a Memorial Day cookout. The day was really nice. My legs were so swollen and sore it was hard for me to get up out of a chair so Carmen made me a plate and I stayed put. Despite the pain, I really enjoyed the day. By the time we ready to go, I was pretty much immobile.

Tuesday morning, Carmen carried me into the doctor's office. All of my joints were screaming. My head throbbed as did my neck. My legs swelled up even tighter than the previous day. I was unable to walk, to dress myself, or do anything for myself. Carmen had to do everything for me, including helping me in the bathroom.

When we got to the doctor's office, they drew blood and put me on anti-inflammatories, and pain meds. They sent me home unable to diagnose what was wrong with me. We went back to Wags. Even though it was warm out, I huddled under my quilt shivering, in a chair, at the shop. Dad and Mom came and got me shortly after we arrived back at Wags, as there was no way I was getting up that ladder to bed. They took me home with them. I stayed with Mom and Dad for almost two weeks. My stay, in spite of the pain, was wonderful.

Chapter 13

Last year, 2006, was a really bad year for us. In the span of two weeks in the spring, we lost my Dad's sister Eileen and his brother, Ted. Then it was Carmen's Uncle Sam, in August. Then Nanny, my Mom's Mom, also in August. Mom's brother-in-law, my Uncle Bill, who always said the doctors tried to "get him well enough to die!" passed away in November. And Terry's Ken, also in November. So many funerals, such awful sadness.

Especially Uncle Ted. He had pancreatic cancer. He fought it for 18 months. My Dad's other sister, Callista Mary passed away in February of 2004 of the same horrible disease. My dad and his brother, Paul, are the only surviving children from my dad's family. Dad took Uncle Ted's death especially hard. They were very close. Not only brothers, but best friends as well.

Uncle Ted stepped in to be best man at my parents wedding when my dad's best man got shipped off by the army right before the wedding. Dad likes to say that he, himself, was the only best man there! Dad returned the favor when Uncle Ted married Aunt Alice. Over the years, Mom and Dad and Aunt Alice and Uncle Ted were always doing something together. They regularly went to dinner, or for coffee. The four of them took many vacations together, or drives, or whatever. They just so enjoyed each other's company.

Our extended family went to mass together as one big family. It would be Aunt Alice, Uncle Ted and their kids. Aunt Eileen and her kids. My Dad and Mom and my siblings. Eventually all of us kids had children of our own, so our pew space grew! We always sat on the north side of the church, four rows back. We take up two or more pews, depending on who shows up.

As all of us kids got older and did our own things after mass, Aunt Alice, Uncle Ted and Mom and Dad would go to breakfast together. I don't think too many days went by without them at least talking on the phone. They went to Hawaii and Cancun on vacations, among other places, and then there were the annual men's golf trips.

Dad and Uncle Ted bowled on the same team for many years, and they were good. The two of them looked alike, so much so that CJ wrapped himself around Uncle Ted's legs one night at the bowling allies thinking it was his grandpa. Uncle Ted didn't mind, he just hugged him back. At our church, Dad and Uncle Ted did a perpetual adoration in the prayer chapel. Someone would be in the chapel who prayed for an hour, every hour, twenty-four hours a day, seven days a week. Dad and Uncle Ted would be there at crazy hours in the morning for their shift. Uncle Ted was a Eucharistic

Minister and Dad was an usher and alms collector at church as well.

So, as I said, Dad took the loss of Uncle Ted very badly. Shortly after the loss of his brother, Dad developed shingles. I really believe it was due to the stress of losing so much in such a short period of time. I didn't go see Dad as much as I wanted to because I was dealing with so much crap of my own.

I didn't need for my dad to see me like that. I didn't want to increase his burden. He had a tough time with the shingles. It's not something to mess with, that's for sure. Shingles are very painful and debilitating. I wish I could have brought him some relief.

Mom and Dad brought me home with them that Tuesday after Memorial Day. I believe that they needed me as much as I needed them. I was a distraction. Something to do out of their daily routine. I know I needed them.

I was on the couch in the living room with my quilt, my anti-inflammatory and pain meds. The pain meds made me really sleepy, which was good as I slept great and needed to sleep. Dad and I watched television during the day and talk. Or I'd sleep. Mostly, I slept. Mom would bring us lunch, always on "good bread", and she would be busy around the house, stopping every few minutes to see if I was okay or I needed anything. Dad would read the paper, never too far out of ear shot.

In the evening, Mom made dinner, but before dinner we had a" little cheese and crackers", then dinner, and later dessert. I was spoiled! They had to help me off the couch to use the bathroom as I couldn't do it myself. In the morning, Mom would make me breakfast and help me to the bathroom to get cleaned up. I could stand in the shower for a little while. Getting in and out of the shower was a chore.

Mom washed my hair for me in the kitchen sink like she did when I was little. It was sweet. One morning, she commented that it had been a long time since she washed my hair. She brushed my hair out for me, ever so gently as even my hair hurt, and helped me get dressed. It's amazing what you take for granted when you have it and how much you miss it when it's gone. I am so lucky to have my Mom!

At night, after dinner, Dad and I watched the Yankees game and Mom read. First we'd watch Jeopardy, as I am a freak about that show. Carmen says I am "smart, Jeopardy smart". Yup, that's me. A plethora of useless knowledge! I do love that show! Eventually, Mom would go up to bed and Dad, well, he slept in his recliner next to the couch I slept on in the living room.

We'd watch the game, and talk until one of us fell asleep. It was one of the best times of my life, and even though the circumstance, I wouldn't change my time with them for anything in the world.

As I got better, Dad and I sat in the back yard swing and enjoyed the day.

Sometimes we talked about the contrails from jets flying overhead. Sometimes we just sat quietly and enjoyed each other's company. Sometimes he'd hold my hand.

With Mom's care and cooking, I put on some of the weight I had lost over the past few months, which was good. I vaguely remember during this time that we went to my sister Mary's house for a cookout. The pain meds really kicked me in the ass, so some stuff is foggy.

What I remember is Mary and the girls put me in the "princess chair" and fed me. At some point my nieces, Elizabeth, better known as Ducky, and Lauren brought me out to the trampoline and I fell asleep on it, in the sun, and it felt wonderful. It was a good day, though any day I spend with them is a good day.

We also swam that day and that felt really good too. The water took all the weight off my joints and I floated around with my girls. Days like that are priceless. So, I got better and eventually went back to the shop.

Carmen called me at Mom and Dad's one day. John and Barb had been to the shop checking on Carmen's progress. As they were preparing to leave, Carmen happened to open in the mailbox and found a letter in it. The letter wasn't properly addressed, someone had stuck it in the mailbox with Carmen and my name on the envelope.

Carmen looked at John, who immediately informed him that our mail wasn't from him. Carmen opened the envelope. Inside was a card with cash in it. The card said it wasn't a loan, nor was it charity, but that sometimes you just need a hand up. It was from my childhood friend Mary, a gold friend.

Well, what do you say? She knew that we were struggling, but not to the extent. When I called Mary to thank her, she told me she could do it, so she did. I told her I couldn't accept it! She wouldn't hear of it. I can't believe it.

We have been friends since we were little. Our parents have been friends since they were little.

I guess that makes Mary one of my oldest friends, um, maybe one of my longest lasting friendships. That sounds better! But to have her come thru like that? I never expected that. I cannot express the emotions. Still. Just blows my mind. We used the cash for more building supplies and groceries. Thank God for the kindness of a true friend!

Chapter 14

What a change! Carmen and Sammy have been kicking ass! We have stairs! The shower is in, the water heater is in! Amazing! I can't believe how much work they got done while I recuperated! We have a shower!!! I am so happy! It is amazing what you take for granted. A shower! This is huge! And all the hot water I can stand. I can't believe how excited I am about this, but when you don't have it readily accessible, well, I didn't really even think about it before. This makes life here so much more bearable.

I know how difficult the days were for Carmen and Sammy. Carmen called me one day while I was at Mom and Dad's. He and Sammy were battling. We tried to make life as normal as usual for Sam since he is just a freshman in High School. Our whole situation is really hard on Sam. We try to let him do "normal" things so as to make his life better. Sometimes he takes advantage of our situation, and uses it against Carmen. Sam wanted to go do something. Carmen told him no, he needed his help. Sammy talked back. Not good. They were both very overtired and over worked. Their tempers boiled over. They called me.

The call destroyed me. Utter despair took me over. I just sat there and cried. I heard Mom say, "your little girl needs you". Dad came in and sat with me and let me cry. All the pain in my body just spilled out. My dad stayed there, held me and let me cry. Pain, frustration, anger, sadness and profound loss. I couldn't take it anymore.

This is hard. I've always been a daddy's girl, guess I still am. My dad held me and let me get it all out. Just held me tight until I cried myself out. I felt like a deflated balloon. Then I slept. I still don't know what I would do without my mom and dad. Carmen and Sammy made peace and got back to work and got a lot done.

As for Sammy, for a kid his age to step up and help build a business as he did says a lot about who he is. He's in high school. His world has been turned upside down. I know he struggles, I hate it. I feel so guilty. I let him down. Yet, here he is. Working side by side with his father to build something for our future, for his future.

Sammy could go live with CJ, or my parents, but he's here, with us. There were many more fights, some pretty ugly, but they always got back to work. Working and being together all day, every day is not easy. I wasn't there to help.

Irritability comes with exhaustion. Carmen and Sam were both irritable and exhausted. But, they got it together. When the kitties came to stay, our first real guests, they had a lovely room to stay in. It had a small desk over the litter box to keep it discrete, a youth bed, a cat condo, lots of toys and very comfy. The kitty room looked so cute! My men did really well.

At some point between the time that we moved out and the house sold, Carmen called the lawyer representing the bank that held our mortgage. Our home went into foreclosure very quickly after the protection papers "fell thru the cracks". We needed to be told by the bank's counsel why we were not allowed to buy our house back nor was anyone we knew allowed to purchase the house.

Carmen and I were told, as we sat in our truck, the phone on speaker, that "even if you walked into this office with a suitcase full of money, we would not sell your house back to you!" The bank lawyer continued to tell us that our attorney had cost his client so much time and money that there was no way, no way, that we would ever get our house back. They would see to it that we never did. Ok. So now we knew. We called Bill and let him know the status.

Pure devastation. I can't put into words how that made us feel. No one should ever be talked to the way this man talked to us. No one should ever be treated like that. No one should ever make another person feel the way we felt, hopeless... Carmen and I then realized that that is why our neighbor could not buy our house.

The bank knew he was our neighbor, and probably a friend, so they denied his offer, and took one for less money, and with stipulations.

I want to go home but now I never can because the house is sold. And to top it off, the woman that is going to live in my house believes everything she hears about what happened to us, none of which came from us. Everyone thinks they know, but they don't. They don't know how hard we worked to get our bills paid. How we tried to keep everything normal for our boys. How much we scraped and scrambled to try and save our business.

Some people think we just sat and watched everything happen to us, and did nothing. Nothing could be further from the truth. I feel that Carmen and I are falling apart to boot. I don't know if I will survive this. "If He leads you to it, He'll bring you through it". Hmmm. Don't know so much about that. Don't think I'll make it through this. All I do is cry. Two-thirty am. As usual, since I've been back from Mom and Dad's, I'm wide awake.

Chapter 15

I feel better than I did earlier, but anything is better than that! We took in our first guests on Monday. Two kitties and tonight, they are actually being quiet. I can see this actually working out okay, but I don't want to say it out loud. Elton John's song "Someone Saved My Life Tonight" is in my head.

I'm selling my drums. I'm not happy about selling them, but this is what you do to survive. Hopefully they will be gone tomorrow so we can get supplies. We had to stop at Alex and Linda's house after having dinner at Tom and Lisa's tonight.   I felt so angry to see our house next door! Rage, sadness, sorrow, loss, all rolled into one. Oh yeah, and embarrassment too.

It's such a long tale to tell, "How I lost my home". So unbelievable. This life still doesn't seem real to me. It's hard staying here all the time. Art, a former teacher of mine and good friend, offered us his house for 3 weeks while he's in California. Lisa asked us again to stay there. So nice of them, but they can't understand that we still have to be here, and, for me at least, it would be harder to come back here. I love them for making the offer.

Being at Dad and Mom's was great. Even though I was sick and hurt, I was so comfortable. I think Mom and Dad liked having me there too. I want to go back with them, but how easy would it be to never come back to the shop? To stay where it is safe and not face this?? Being at Mom and Dad's was like being in a cocoon. Enveloped in care and love. Being taken care of, every need met. Yeah it was pretty good. Pretty great in fact, but then, Carmen and Sammy need me.

Carmen is a bit cranky. The stress takes its toll on him in a different way than on me. It's not good. If building this doesn't kill Carmen, his anger will.

You can't get back what you've lost in this situation. The house is one thing. Your sense of being is something else.

I've lost a lot of me during this time. I question my faith that was once so strong. I need to write this. It is cathartic. When I used to pray, it was my quiet time in conversation with God. One on one. It was always a two way conversation. I now feel that I am talking to someone, but that someone isn't who I thought it was. I am being tricked into talking to someone who isn't there to help me succeed, but to fail. I am being taunted and mocked by whomever is stealing my prayers.

My prayers are being intercepted. They are not being heard by God. Man, this is hard to put into words. I feel like God wants to come through, but something is stopping Him. Does this even make any sense? I used to trust that voice, my gut, my God. Now I'm afraid to because I feel my prayers are being stolen.

I tried to wish on a star the other night and it wouldn't come. No wish. I feel I have nothing to wish for now. Someone more worthy than I should get the wish. We have no home, no cash flow and I can't wish. I don't have it in me anymore.

I used to stand on my porch at night before I went to bed. I talked to everyone in my life who had passed. While looking at the stars, I would hear them talk back to me just as clearly as if they were right next to me. Their voices are gone now. The sky is so beautiful and I get nothing. I keep trying and no one answers. I want to scream out my frustration. I cry for my loss. I cry all the time. I'm angry, disappointed and miserable. This is NOT what I wanted for a life for us.

I'm hurt. Mentally and physically. I somehow need to get back to who I am as a person. I feel so stupid. I was a dreamer and I believed what I heard in my head that everything would be just fine. "Somehow this will all work out, my house will be mine, we won't have to move out, I'm gonna prove them wrong!" I had said those words. Didn't happen. We are homeless, never in a million years did I think that would be me. So, that makes me a stupid dreamer. And dead wrong too.

The house is sold. No more dreams, wishes, hope or prayers. I'm done. "You are always smiling!" I got that all the time. That's when I thought I had a relationship with God. I talked to God like He was an old friend, I had since I was little. I remember the day that I decided He wasn't someone to be afraid of, but someone that cared about me.

I told God everything, even though He saw everything, predestined it for me. I was just walking the game board that He set for me and He was watching me play the real game of Life. Game over. Tilt. Something. Now I feel like 'who the hell do you think you are?' Why was I being all self- important? There are so many other people in the world, it's not all about me! He has so many more prayers to answer. So many more people to talk to in the world.

I thought it was one more of the mysteries of my faith, like how God is one man and yet, He is The Father, The Son and The Holy Spirit. For that matter, that Jesus died on the cross and rose again. These were just "givens" to me. I don't question that. It is what it is. Faith unseen.

I miss that relationship so much. It is so quiet now. I don't hear choir music in my head anymore either. It was there all the time and I would joyously sing out at the top of my lungs and not care who heard me. I don't sing out anymore because that joy is not there. That song is gone. Replaced by what? Black. Just black.

How do you get thru this pain? How, how, how?? I just don't know. I've been writing for almost an hour now. I'm going try to sleep. I'm going to try to pray and not get a busy signal this time. And, hope that my prayers are going to the one to whom they are intended and not intercepted by a mocking presence!

Chapter 16

Building has progressed, slow but steady. We have rooms up and had a few dogs and cats here, mostly friend's pets. My friend Mary brought her two West Hyland White Terriers, Maddie and Sydney here for a stay. The dogs give us sort of a test run to see what we need to change and what we don't. It appears that we are doing okay.

We have had a lot of people stop by to see what we are building. Carmen, Sammy or I give a quick tour to explain what it is we are going to have here at Wags. We have received very positive comments and feedback, which is always good. We've had dinner at Tom and Lisa's a bunch of times, thank God for them. Takes our minds off things for a bit.

Tom, Lisa, Tommy and Christopher are in Rhode Island now for their annual trip. I'm happy they got to go. They have no idea how much their kindness means to us. Someday I hope I can repay them.

Oh, and we got a shih-tzu puppy from June. We went to see the puppies like new dads in a nursery. We weren't supposed to get a shih-tzu. June called and said her pair had a litter of pups. She had one female that someone was supposed to take, but the family changed their mind. June asked if we would take her so she wouldn't have to advertise again. Yeah, okay, sure. We'll come look at her.

Never say you are going to "just look" at a puppy, because it never turns into a "just look". Admit it, the "just look" is going to be a "go pick one out"! We saw Lola. She was adorable. Two weeks later, we brought Lola home.

We introduced her to Wiley, not really sure how he was going to like this, but he immediately took her as his little sister. Lola and Wiley sniffed each other. She submitted by rolling on to her back. Wiley let her figure him out and then he tried to engage her in play, to which she happily obliged. They are sister and brother of a different mother!

Lola's littermate, Bella began day care shortly after. She was adopted by our friends, Bridget and Nick. Carmen picks her up in the morning so she can hang out with Lola and Wiley. The three of them play, eat, and nap together. Play time is great.

Wiley lays down and the girls jump all over and on top of him. He opens his mouth to protest and one of them will stick their little head in his mouth! He is so gentle with them. He fakes his displeasure, loving every minute of it.

When someone comes into Wags, I tell Wiley, Lola and Bella to "kennel up" so they aren't in the way. In they go, into Wiley's big crate that is full of all of his favorite blankets and some toys. They just wait and nap until it is time to come back out. The girls have been gnawing on his bottom lip to the extent that it is raw, but he doesn't care. They are his girls. He is their big brother, protector, and chew toy.

Lola and Bella follow Wiley everywhere. If the girls get to rambunctious, Wiley puts a paw out and onto their backs, and puts them to the floor. Very gently of course. That big paw can break up any fight. If they fight over a treat or toy, he separates them this way. When we give Wiley a cookie, he breaks the cookie up with his teeth into little pieces and drops it on the floor for the girls.

He loves to share with them because they give him kisses afterward and cuddle up against him to nap. In the evening, Bella goes home and Wiley and Lola have dinner together. They go for a walk and later off to bed.

As the girls got older, they found that they could grab Wiley by his tail and he would drag them around the floor. They jump up on his face until he lays down and rolls over on his back. He then complains like an old bear in faked displeasure. The girls love this. They jump on him even more until they all tire out and nap in a heap on the floor or in Wiley's crate.

The crate door is always left open for them to go in and rest. Bella eventually stopped coming every day for daycare, but she still comes in for a stay or a Wiley fix now and then. The festivities start all over again as soon as Bella arrives. She still adores her "big brother".

Chapter 17

July 16th, 2007

   I think that's the date, not really sure. I took Sammy to his friend Mikey's house. As we passed our house, I noticed there was a car in the driveway. Seeing that really disturbed me. I feel, sometimes, that I don't want to live in my house. Sometimes I think I don't want to go back there, but I do. I miss my house so much. I hate being broke, we sank all we had into this, sold everything, Carmen's tools and tool box, my drums, my jewelry, our furniture, the Mustang, all gone at "drastic discount prices!". That statement would be funny if it weren't true.

   We work all day, every day with the only break being an occasional dinner with Tom and Lisa. It's really hard, but we have to keep going or we will fail and that is not going to happen. We seem to be surrounding ourselves with good people. Meeting clients who are good and true. Makes our job a lot easier. We should be officially open soon.

Matt, a reporter, is doing a story on us for the Syracuse Post Standard. That should bring us some new customers. He originally got a hold of us because of the floats for the Marcellus Old Home Days Parade. Carmen and Tom do one every year, one that is always decided upon after a few Jack and Cokes and usually only a few days prior to the parade.

Their first brilliant float idea had them dressed as a Nun, Carmen, and Tom as a Bishop. We figured if we could get past Mom with the float, we would continue on the parade route. If not, we would turn down a side street and exit the parade. Lisa and I had them in the back of our decorated truck with Gregorian Chants played out through speakers. Carmen, Tom and our boys tossed candy to the kids.

First of all, we hadn't even registered to be in the parade. We just jumped in ahead of the snowmobile club float that Bridget and Nick were on. When we got to Mom, she started laughing and we knew we could proceed.

We arrived at the viewing stand where a local radio station personality was announcing the floats and he had to pause. Announcing us as the snowmobile club, he looked up from his notes, realized who it was, as we had all gone to school together, and he too began to laugh as he announced that it was Tom and Carmen! We were a hit.

Throughout the following year Tom, Lisa, Carmen and I, had to field questions as to what the next year would bring. No one knew until the last minute because we didn't know until then either. In the years that followed Carmen and Tom dressed up as Cheerleaders, complete with uniforms. They were lovely. The "girls" were asking to get the cheerleading squad up again as it hadn't

been in a few years. It worked. Our
school has a cheerleading squad again. I
don't know if they really helped the
cheerleaders cause, but I like to think it
did!

   Another year my husband and my
brother were bathing beauties dressed in
god awful, women's bathing suits. They
were the "Nine Mile Yacht Club". Nine
Mile being the name of the creek that
runs thru town. The two of them, in
Walmart, trying on women's bathing
suits. The clerk in the changing room
kind of looked at them and said it was ok
but, that they had to come out and
model them once they were on!

   I think she thought it would embarrass
them. Um, not really. It would take a
lot more than a bathing suit to
embarrass those two! We hitched our
boat up to our truck, stuck Carmen and
Tom in their lovely attire and make-up in
the boat with our sons, and off we went.
Once again, the hit of the parade!

For our "Redneck Weddin" theme, Lisa and I dressed Carmen and Tom in Hill Billy attire. We drove them in our work RV. We had signs and cans attached to the back bumper. All of the signs were misspelled. The cans we used were empty beer cans. Tom dressed up as the new bride for that one. He was so purdy! The happy couple hung out of the windows, waving and tossing candy to the crowd.

One year, Carmen got really ambitious and decided to do the "Death Mobile" from the film Animal House. He got an old Lincoln Town Car and took a saw to it. Carmen, with the help of CJ, Sammy, and Tommy got it to bare bones and then began rebuilding. Tom went and got candy to throw to the crowd and the needed accessories.

The transformation looked similar to what took place in the film, with less sophisticated tools. Carmen designed and built a turret on top and a hatch in the trunk like the one John Belushi popped out of in the film. Carmen attached an air whistle on the turret and Faber's head was mounted on the front. Faber was the founder of Faber College, the fictional university in the film.

That float was beautiful! The "Death Mobile" looked so much like the original that we were contacted by a local radio station wanting to use it for their Animal House Reunion party at the New York State Fairgrounds. Dewayne Jessie, who played Otis Day of "Otis Day and the Knights" in the movie, was guest of honor. He told Carmen that his car was the closest replica he had seen. Dewayne signed the turret for us and had pictures taken with the car. Pretty cool.

Matt had seen pictures of the car and had heard about Carmen and Tom. He wanted to do a human interest story for the paper. He came in to meet us at the shop and got down to the business about the floats. When he was done, Matt asked about what we were building here, at Wags. We filled him in and he was intrigued. Matt wanted another story, so we gave him one. The story about the parade floats was in our Neighbor's section of the paper, complete with a picture of the car.

For the Wags story, Matt wanted more information. He brought the Wags story to his editor. The editor had him do more research on kennels. Matt made phone calls. He did internet searches. He found that places that said they were doing what we are, were, in fact, the same as what was already out there. Matt really did his homework. Some kennels had lovely foyers and play areas. As soon as you get to the rooms for the guests, they were just kennels and not at all a room. The other places were nothing like he had seen at Wags.

Matt came back to Wags, took a bunch of photos and interviews and wrote a story. It wasn't put in the local Neighbor's section as we thought. Wags was front page news, top story for July

31st, 2007. We were big news!   Now the real work begins!

Carmen and I had to go into Syracuse to get our paperwork in order on the day the article came out. Sammy manned the phones at Wags. Wow, what a response! Sam would no sooner hang up the phone from one person, and it would ring immediately with another. He was overwhelmed! I knew that there was a need for a place like this, but to this extent, I had no idea. Calls aren't just local either. Calls came in from all over. We took reservations in no time at all.

Our official opening date is August 10th, but people want us now! Awesome. Maybe we'll be okay. I've been too busy lately to really dwell on the house, which is good. Carmen and Sammy still get on each other's nerves, but we haven't killed each other yet. I think I have come to terms with the fact that we are going to be here for the long haul and living here is going to be a part of it. I'm okay with that reality.

We justified our staying here with the town board. We are open 24 hours a day. Someone has to, in fact, be here, so it's kind of a grey area. We had to explain that what difference does it make if someone sleeps in one of the beds in a room or upstairs in a bed? Someone has to be here for our guests in case one of them needs something! Some dogs can't go all night without going out. I just feel better knowing someone is here, just in case.

The kitchen/utility room is done. We have our washer and dryer from the house to keep things clean. So glad we hung on to them. They are paid for. We have a refrigerator which helps when guests bring in raw diets. We don't have a stove yet, can't afford one, but we do have the grill and microwave. I am grateful for the microwave as guests bring in food that needs to be heated up. We want to make this as much like home for them as possible.

I have become very humble of late. I am grateful for the smallest kindness. I thought I always was. Our current situation has brought my gratefulness to a whole new level. When we were doing well, people would come to us for things. One Easter, they were short hams for the Easter Basket give away at our church. The baskets are for local families in need. We gave the church a check to get what they needed. It was a great feeling for me.

Afterward, I felt kind of guilty because it gave me so much pleasure to write that check! I don't know if that makes sense. I guess because I had always heard "give 'til it hurts". This didn't hurt at all! It was a rush handing that check over and knowing that someone would have a better day because of it.

Carmen adopted a family one Christmas, and hired a man to play Santa to deliver their gifts. Carmen took our boys shopping for the woman and her two daughters while I was at work. CJ and Sammy loved it, saying they were helping a "poor" family. I told them they weren't poor, just having a hard time just then. They picked out toys for the little girls and a teddy bear for the mom. They went to the grocery store and bought not only their Christmas dinner and all the fixings, but enough food to last them a week. Again, the rush.

Our employees, we housed them and fed them. Our friends in need, we took care of things when there was a death or illness in the family. We brought food, cleaned, or did whatever we could do. When a friend was in need, we jumped to help any way we could. Being there is what you are supposed to do. For anyone.

It is our responsibility to our fellow human beings, and as Christians. Not something we thought about. Just something we acted on. That is how I was raised. I think it is an excellent way to be raised. I have really good role models. I hope that I am the same for my kids. Check that. I see what they do now and that gives me hope.

We are moving right along with the building. We had carpet installed in the main area and office area and we laid area rugs in all of the rooms. The smaller rugs make for easy clean up, should there be an accident, and also for regular maintenance. Each room has some furniture in it. Two of our rooms have the boy's old bunk beds in them.

Furniture has been donated to Wags by a couple of CJ's friends. The furniture was from their dorm rooms at college. I found ping pong balls in one couch. I was unaware that "beer pong" is an accredited course! We cover everything in plastic and then in fresh linens. Makes it homey. Our guests like their rooms. I know this because they are quiet.

It's amazing the difference between here and kennels that I have been to. You can actually have a normal conversation in here, even with all the rooms filled. Why? Because the "kids", as I call them, are comfortable. They don't have other dogs staring at them and barking at them.

They can't see each other, but they can see the TV! They don't have to protect their stuff, or their area because it's not theirs. They don't have to protect their owner because they aren't here. Our guests can take a cue from Wiley and relax. The calm and quiet are awesome! I didn't expect this.

I thought there would be a lot of barking and whining because that is what I had observed at other kennels. Not here. Our guests are on vacation here and they know it. They don't have to work. We take them outside for walks. We clean up their room for them and change their linens. Housekeeping. We give them fresh food and water as per their schedule. Water is changed all the time. Room service for our guests. They have play time in the main area and can get whatever toy they want out of the toy box. Then, they retire to their room.

At eleven am it is absolutely silent in here. I don't know if it's due to an internal clock or what, but every dog takes a nap at that time. We can talk on the phone or have a normal conversation, and there is no noise. It is so cool! Another affirmation that we really needed to do this for the pet loving community!

I still wake up every day with achy joints. Nothing showed up on the blood work. They ran tests for Lupus, fibromyalgia, arthritis and God knows what else. My nurse practitioner and Angel on Earth, Nancy, is pretty stumped. We discussed what had been going on with us. We think my illness may have been a reaction to all the stress I have been under. Ya think! Our bodies react in strange ways to stress.

Maybe this was the way my body handled it. So, I take my pain and anxiety meds. They help to some degree. The only thing that would really help is being home and for none of this to have happened. But, this whole nightmare did happen. This is my reality.

I think I am getting better about accepting my new life.

Seeing how my guests react to being here, and how happy their families are to have them here, makes me know that there are no coincidences. I am exactly where I am supposed to be right now. As much as it sucks sometimes, this is, as it should be. Knowing that helps. It really does. And with the love and support of my family and a few good friends, we'll be okay. We just keep on going, don't quit.

Chapter 18

Carmen built a deck by the front door, across from the office in our entryway. It's a good greeting area. The dogs like hanging out there. Lola and Bella play on the deck a lot with Wiley. We had a guest named Gretchen come in and she and Lola were playing up there. They had gotten in to something, and I called them on it. Both of them turned around at the same time to look at me. They were so busted! Lola is pretty good with the guests. Wiley is amazing. He greets everyone.

All dogs that come in meet Wiley. He's sort of a litmus test. If Wiley sniffs them and walks away, the guest can stay. With a few, the hair on his back has gone up and we know it might not be a good fit. We will, however, give the dog a chance. If it works out and they have a good stay, great. If not, we won't ask them back.

I should have paid more attention when Joe, the Weimeriner came in. I'm changing his name to protect the innocent! Wiley didn't seem too pleased that he was here, but we gave it a shot. The dog obviously had issues. Joe came in with more medications than I had ever seen for a dog. No problem. I had his schedule. One of the meds was a tranquilizer. That should have been a red flag.

Joe's family had rescued him. I respect that. He was the only one that had survived from his litter. I had had a Weimeriner and he was great. This would be a breeze! I took him out for a walk. Joe did his business, and we walked around the yard. I told him to sit. Good so far.

I told him "down" and lowered my hand to the down position. Nope. Joe's eyes rolled to the back of his head and he lunged. He caught me on my right palm under my ring finger and re-bit on my thumb. He was going to go for me again. I yelled "off" calmly and sternly to show I was still in control and to snap him out of whatever trance he appeared to be in. Joe backed off. I headed back inside with him.

We kept the front door of Wags locked to keep it secure in the building for our guests. As it was locked now, and blood dripped down my hand, I calmly knocked on the door for Carmen to let me in. He took one look at the blood and freaked out. He just stood there and looked at me. I calmly asked him to open the door and I walked Joe back to his room. He went in to his room fine, but as I went to close the door, he tagged my ankle.

Carmen was beside himself. He hates to see anyone hurt, let alone me with all of this blood. I calmed him down and went into the kitchen and washed off my injury. It was ugly. Probably needed stitches too, but I didn't need that. We have only been open a short time and to have to have a dog taken out of here, that wouldn't do. I cleaned the wound really well, put antibacterial ointment on it and wrapped it up. Then I cried. I think more because I was disappointed than hurt, although it was throbbing. Just add it to the other throbbing, no worries.

Carmen called Joe's family and told them what happened and they said okay and they'd see us on Sunday. Hmmm. This was Friday. Okay? Their dog had only been with us a few hours. Carmen also called Joe's vet to make sure, double check, that he was up to date on his rabies vaccine. He was, but he did indeed have issues.

The vet tech was the one that told us that Joe was the only survivor of the litter and the tech also told us Joe had "shaken puppy syndrome" Similar to shaken baby syndrome, it causes neurological problems with the dog. I, in fact, had witnessed one of the issues.

I can't imagine keeping a dog like that, with kids in the family, not to mention in the neighborhood where he is walked. That is a walking disaster! What if Joe got a hold of a child??? Scary. We ended up giving him one of his tranquilizers as he started tearing the room apart. Joe destroyed the carpet, dug at the walls, which are wood, and dug up the screen door to his room. He literally ran up my walls until the meds kicked in. There was no calming him. Finally, he slept.

His parents came and got him on Sunday. We stupidly agreed to try Joe one more time. We will give anyone a second chance. Joe came in again, this time sedated. That is no life, having to be sedated all the time. He was fine, until he came out of it, and again, he freaked. We put Joe in a room, different from his last stay, to see if it would make a difference. The room has tiled floor and we took the furniture out. It still was very comfortable as we put down his bed and a few toys and an extra blanket. As I said, he was fine, dopey, but fine.

During the night, Joe's meds wore off. He pushed against his door so hard that he could reach the carpet outside of his door. He dug and dug at it until he tore up what was there. This carpet was attached to the wall to wall that was in the main room. The carpet that we had just installed.

In the morning, Carmen took Joe out for a walk. I wasn't going near him. As Carmen tried to get Joe back in his room, he bit Carmen. The dog went home the next day. Joe was the first dog banned from Wags. I commend his family for saving him, but when they knew of his problems and the potential for harm, no, I wag my finger at them.

Counting on that many pills to live a normal life is no way for a dog to live. It's not fair to the dog or his family. They were very lucky it was me that got bit and not someone who would seek some sort of compensation for "pain and suffering" and a scar on their palm!

We went from Joe, to Freyja. In Norse mythology, Freyja is the goddess of love and beauty. Freyja lives up to her name. She is an 11 year old keeshond. She is wonderful. Freyja is short, stocky and very wooly. She reminds me of a caterpillar. Happy to be anywhere at any time, she is a real joy to have here. Freyja and Lola hit it off immediately. They spend most of the day on the deck as people come in and out and tell them how cute they are. She has a little problem with urinary incontinence, but she is worth every clean up that we do.

We are open for business, but are still working on the building. The first time Freyja came in was a busy week, so no construction was being done. Being that this is a quiet week, we are trying to get some siding up behind the deck up front. When that is done, we'll put deck chairs up there and make it campy looking. After closing for the day, Carmen decided to finish up the siding.

He got the screw gun out and the screws and siding and got to work. Sam and I were feeding our guests dinner and they were all in their rooms. Carmen no sooner started the screw gun than a howling started in one of the rooms. I followed the sound, and there was Freyja, head back in a full out howl! It was hysterical! I told Carmen to do it again. Again, as soon as he started, Freyja started too. We had to finish the wall so he continued on, and every time he fired up the screw gun Freyja would howl!

We laughed at this silly dog and she was loving it! She knew she was being funny! At one point I told him to stop and then told Freyja that "Carmen is going to use the screw gun"! She put her head back and howled at that! Her tail wagged so! Freyja hopped about as we let her out of her room to see what was going on and making that sound. Every time we either told her Carmen was going to use, or that he did use the screw gun, she would howl. So funny! And brilliant. They are so much smarter than we give them credit for. During that week, Carmen did more work with his screw gun and every time without fail, Freyja helped!

Chapter 19

The phone rings with regularity since the newspaper article. We have received calls from individuals with very recognizable names. I don't put much stock into someone's name, or who they may "be". I can't form an opinion about a person by their name. I have to meet a person to get a sense of who they are before I can form my own opinion. I like to see how someone treats others, and how they carry themselves first. I need to believe that when I meet someone new, that that person has a good heart. Until a person proves me wrong, that is all I can do.

I have never understood why people put others on a pedestal, or, conversely, treat them wrongly because of something they heard. It's not fair to the person or to myself. I could miss out on meeting a great person or making a wonderful friend if I don't at least give them a chance. I'd rather regret a choice I made than regret not making a choice at all.

Such was the case with a woman I will call Grace. I will use that name because Grace is a blessing, and to me, she is just that. After speaking with her on the phone, Grace came in with her cocker spaniel, Buck, for a stay. It was obvious the affection the two have for each other. Buck is black, with a stub of a tail that does not stop wagging. Grace is pretty, stylish and petite. She is lovely, personable, and down to earth. Qualities I admire. As icing on the cake, she is also very funny. I liked them both immediately.

Grace left Buck with us for his first stay. He came in and met everyone and made himself at home. Buck is kind of a hug hog, but wasn't nasty about it. He just made it clear the world was made just for his pleasure. We also quickly learned that Buck has bad separation anxiety as he would howl when left alone at night in his room. We tried leaving him in the main room, on the couch with Wiley at night, but, then too, he howled. Upstairs Buck came, to sleep next to my side of the bed on a huge overstuffed pillow. He had picked his spot.

During the day, Buck hung out on the couch and watched TV with Wiley in the main area, our living room for the guests. At night, Buck was back upstairs for bed. It worked out great. Grace came and picked him up after her trip. Buck was so happy to see her. He let her know he did great on his first stay and that he had so much fun!

The reunion is one of the best parts about Wags. The reunion between guest and 'parent' when they get picked up. I love the reaction of the parent when they see a happy dog come out instead of one cowering or miserable. Grace was very happy. And happy to see that Buck did, indeed, do so well! Then something unusual happened. We got our first tip!

Grace had no idea it was our first, nor did she know how much it meant to us. It was a pat on the back, a "well done". I could survive on that if I didn't need to eat! Carmen was always a good tipper. I thought I knew how much it meant to someone to get that extra acknowledgement. It is, in fact, pretty great!

In September of 2007, CJ was laid off from his job. It was great while he worked because he helped us out financially. He didn't have to, but he did. That's what kind of kid he is. I don't know how I got so lucky.

My mom wished a kid like me, on me, for so long. It's amazing to me that I ended up with my two boys! CJ started looking for a new job. He would stop in to visit and give us a hand between job hunts. I wanted him with us because we needed him, but we couldn't afford him.

Later in the month, as he still couldn't find a job, he came to Wags. He has helped us build more rooms as we already need them. I had to have surgery in late September, to move the ulnar nerve in my elbow. The accident Carmen and I were in in February caused the nerve to be pinched between the medial epicondyle, which is a bump of bone on the inside of the elbow. The nerve caused the pain and numbness in my right hand. Carmen wanted to take me out to see The Rhythm Method play in downtown Syracuse for my birthday, so bandaged up and all, we went.

It was a lot of fun. We went with our friends, John and Jill. Carmen and I had met John and Jill through our mutual friend Jodi, who sings with the Rhythm Method. We have been friends since that first introduction a few years ago. Going out to see the Rhythm Method with them is always fun, but not so great with my arm wrapped up. I got bumped into, but it was okay. Jill started running defense for me!

Carmen and I needed a good night out. We didn't stay out very long, and I went back and stayed with Mom and Dad again. It was lovely. This time I could sleep in my old room because I can climb stairs better now. They didn't have to work so hard either. I stayed a couple of days so I could rest and I did indeed do that.

We are still doing construction at Wags. We now have part of the other side of our building, so more rooms are going up by the stairs. Speaking of stairs, we carpeted the upstairs too, and have our bed up there and our dressers. Sammy has his futon in his room and he sleeps on that. Our room is the first one you walk into, then thru the bathroom, and into Sammy's. It's all kind of open, no doors, but it will do.

CJ, Sammy and their friends pile into Sammy's room to watch movies and play games. I thought that when we moved out of the cabin that the boy's friends would stop coming, but no, they still do. The walls aren't even really walls on the inside. We use all of the building material for the hotel so our living area is totally unfinished and yet, they still come! The boy's friends lend a hand every now and then. And June pops in whenever she has time. Every extra pair of hands really helps.

We put a faux roof- front over the rooms to make the motel look more like an outdoor building. Looks great. June and I held the roof frames up while the boys nailed them in. At night I am so tired. Come to think of it, I'm tired all the time. Must be part of whatever is going on with my legs. I sleep a lot still. Most nights I fall asleep really quick and soundly only to be wide awake a few hours later.

Insomnia has its benefits. Having "mom ears" does too. Our room looks over the motel so we can hear if any of our guests barks or cries. I am the one that usually gets up with a guest that needs to go out, as Carmen and Sammy are up early for the morning shift. I rather enjoy the midnight walks. It's so quiet here at night, so peaceful. We have lights on around our building but it's still dark enough that the stars are really bright.

I had a guest out at around 3:30 one morning, and a New York State Trooper car pulled in. The Trooper asked if everything was okay, I told him it was. He said that they will check on us when patrolling out our way. I thanked him and he told me he'd drive around our building before he left. I thought that was great! Now Carmen won't worry when I'm out in the middle of the night walking a guest.

Midnight potty walks are a part of what sets us apart from other boarding facilities. I know the dogs appreciate it. When I bring a guest back in, they get a hug and kiss and go right back to bed. Just like kids. My kids. They are all becoming my kids. My sons are my boys. My guests are my kids. I am so grateful they are here.

Thanksgiving arrived. Mom and Dad, Mary, Rob and the girls, were going to Tom and Lisa's for dinner. We couldn't attend because we have guests. A full house, thank God. Lisa, Tommy, and Christopher, brought dinner to Wags for us. Ducky and Lauren came too. The food was so good.

I really thought this was going to be just another day at work. Thanksgiving just wasn't going to be the same. Every cent we make goes into building supplies, so there is nothing extra for celebrations. We were just going to have sandwiches. Having my family bring us dinner was a big deal. It was really great to see them. We have missed a lot being here. I am so glad they came. I am truly grateful and I am truly thankful for how far we have come.

Chapter 20

Around Christmastime, Carmen went to see our attorney, Bill. He wanted to tell him that we had decided not to proceed with our lawsuit against him for "dropping the ball" on our house. I asked Carmen to wait a minute as I wanted to give him a note to give to Bill. I grabbed a Christmas card.

I wrote in the card that we would not be pursuing litigation against him. I had to let the negative feelings go, and reliving it would not help. I told Bill that if it weren't for what happened, we wouldn't be where we are. No coincidences. We are where we are supposed to be right now. It's not my ideal situation, but I can see we are making a difference. I forgave him. I had to forgive him so I could move on.

Carmen and CJ went to get us a Christmas tree. Just a little one to put on the deck. It's more for me than anything. I love a fresh tree. At this point it is a luxury, not a necessity. For the sake of moral, however, it is a necessity.

They went to a Christmas tree farm, not far from Wags. Since Christmas is only a couple of days away, they were pretty low on choices. There was one perfect one, but it was huge and expensive. Carmen told the guy that he only had forty bucks to spend and he'd have to cut this one down to fit. The guy took Carmen's forty dollars and he and CJ brought that ginormous tree back to Wags.

Instead of cutting it down to a reasonable size, they set it up. That tree is about 14 feet tall! It's on the deck. It looks perfect. I cried, no surprise. It made me so happy. I dug out our decorations and put the kids homemade ones, the ones with their little "squishy faces" on them, on the tree with the lights. Our tree is beautiful. I hope they know that tree is going to stay up for as long as it has needles!

Christmas was so busy! We had no money for gifts, but we received cards, wine, candy and, homemade cut out cookies, my favorite, from our customers. Grace brought Buck in for a stay and picked him before the Holiday. She gave the boys a nice tip which, they used to buy their girlfriends gifts. If it weren't for Grace, they wouldn't have had a gift to give. She has no idea.

Our customer's thoughtfulness made Christmas special for us. I never expected such kindness, especially since we have only been here a couple of months. None of our customers know what we have been dealing with which makes it even more amazing. None of them know that we started out in here, sleeping in a tent where their kids now play. It really is a shock for me. They have no idea how much I appreciate their thoughtfulness!

Christmas made me realize the impact we are having on people. We must be doing something right. We have had a bunch of guests come back again. Customers rebook when they pick up. That is such a compliment! And a bunch of recommendations too. We have done no advertising, people just hear about us from friends and call.

Questions, questions, questions, and we answer every one. How else will people get a sense of who we are and what we are doing at Wags? People want to be assured that their kids are going to be treated as they are at home. We go beyond that and spoil them! Lots of hugs, kisses and belly rubs here!

New Year's Eve, Carmen and I drove to Rochester to see an Irish band. Sammy stayed and kept an eye on the place. We drove all the way to the venue they were playing, only to find out that the band had cancelled due to an illness. It was a nice ride anyway. We wished each other a Happy New Year on the New York State Thruway, both hoping that it would be a good year. We drove back to the shop. It's still really hard to call this home.

Chapter 21

Monday, March 10th, 2008

I'm going take my time writing this because it's really important. Our dear friend and Carmen's mentor, Richey passed away at 9:15am on Sunday, March 8, 2008. He was truly a compassionate, considerate, sweet man. A gentleman in every sense of the word. Richey gave us so much support and encouragement. By giving us hope and friendship that was so needed at the time, he helped us survive the crash and burn in our lives.

God has gotten two winners in such a short time. Father Joseph Champlin on January 17th, and now Richey. Godspeed to you both and please, because you have favor in Gods eyes, pray for me. I love you and miss you both. I would have traded my life to save yours in an instant.

Father Champlin was pastor at our Church, St. Joseph's on the Hill in Camillus, New York. Not only our priest, he was a family friend. He concelebrated family wedding masses with Father Fred, consoled my parents when Carmen and I eloped. He baptized our children. He was such a part of every major event in our lives.

Father counseled Uncle Ted during his illness despite his own illness. He was in a fight against cancer as well. Father Champlin spent time with Uncle Ted, and the two of them would discuss what was to come. They shared their amazing faith with each other and their trust that God had a reason for their pain and suffering. Everyone loved Father Champlin. It was a sad day when he passed away, but we all knew what awaited him in Heaven. He indeed could join the Communion of Saints!

And then there was Richey. Carmen and I had gone to see Sammy's football game. Richey's grandson was one of

Sammy's teammates. We had briefly met Richey and his wife Diana at a previous game. It was a cold and windy day. The sky was threatening a cold rain. Typical football weather.

Carmen and I had gone up into the announcer's booth at the High School stadium to stay warm because my aunt was filming the game from there. We saw that Richey and Diana shivered in the cold and asked if they wanted to come in and get warm. They quickly accepted our invitation.

Making conversation, Richey asked Carmen what he did. Carmen told him of the log home industry and about our new endeavor, Wags. Richey's response to a pet motel was a chuckle, but he was interested. Anyone that we ever told our idea to, chuckled. Richey and Carmen talked construction, and business between football plays. Carmen had a new friend.

When our former world crumbled, Richey and Diana heard about our situation from their daughter. They came to see Carmen and I as we worked on Wags. We had them come in and we sat, the four of us, on a stack of lumber and talked. Diana is a pistol. Whatever is on her mind, she speaks out loud. She is a riot! I love her blatant honesty.

Diana and Richey asked what had happened to us, and Carmen told them. We had nothing to hide. Our pride had been shattered. We wanted the people that actually cared and didn't assume to know, to really know what went down. We told them about the business, the house, everything. Diana's reply, "Richey, write them a check to get their house back!" We politely thanked them, but refused.

Richey knew our attorney, and was a bit dismayed, but he respected us enough not to push the issue. Carmen told them, "This is our problem and we will fix it. Thank you so much for your concern, but your continued friendship and moral support is all we need." We indeed got that. Richey would stop in, sometimes with Diana, but mostly alone, and comment on Carmen's work. And they would talk.

Richey was such an inspiration to Carmen and such an honest and loving friend. A great mentor. He would walk in to Wags with a "Carmen! Hey!" Then, "look at this! Great job!" I can't believe how far you have come!" Always positive. He always complemented Carmen on his work. A good day was made when Richey came in.

On one visit, Richey asked what we were going to use to cover the plywood we had put up, to make it look as if the motel was outside. Carmen said we might paint it or put siding up. "I have some old siding at the shop and some old display windows if you want them", Richey told him. Carmen said okay, and we were told they would be dropped off in a few days.

The next day a truck rolled in with a huge load of siding and a couple of

sample windows. The driver unloaded it all in our foyer and Carmen asked for the bill. The reply we got floored us, "there is no bill". WHAT???? Who does that??? Our answer, Richey. Carmen called him immediately and told him we couldn't take all of this material. Richey insisted that it was, in fact, discontinued. He said "that load was the end of what I had. I can't use it. I can't get anymore, so what good is it to me?"

I still don't believe that. I do believe Richey was an angel on earth. We have a couple of them now! We are having a plaque made honoring Richey to hang in Wags. He was diagnosed with stomach cancer about that time or shortly after. Carmen and I were at Richey and Diana's house for a Christmas party and also a Super Bowl party.

At both, Carmen and Richey would cloister themselves at a table and discuss their upbringing, life, our business. Carmen cherished those times.

One afternoon we went to visit Richey, as we heard he was home after a hospital stay. We didn't know how bad he was at that point, and we brought he, and Diana an upside down pizza. The pizza is made by putting the cheese on first, sauce next, and then parmesan cheese. It's delicious.

We thought that Diana probably wasn't eating much and maybe Richey could have a little. Maybe it would perk up his appetite. He was too sick to have any. We felt really bad. At least Diana enjoyed the pizza. I was glad to see her eat. We had a really nice visit.

On the way back to Wags, Carmen cried. He hated to see his friend suffering so, but Richey was happy to see Carmen. Richey, Diana, Carmen and I had sat in their sun room and talked. Richey asked how we were doing. He sat there with all these medicines, and was so thin, and he asked if we were okay…

On the Friday before Richey passed, we received a call that he was not doing well at all. It was just a matter of time. We had to go see him and thank him again for all he had done for us. Carmen didn't want to go. I had to talk him into going. Carmen didn't think he could handle seeing Richey that sick again.

Richey was so much worse when Carmen and I got to the house. Diana was at the kitchen table going over details for the funeral. We went into Richey's room. His grandson and niece were there. Richey was in bed and I thought we were too late. His breathing was so intermittent.

His grandson and niece kept talking to him and rubbing him to make him breath. It was heartbreaking. Everyone loved this man so. We just stood there and said a silent prayer. We didn't know what else to do.

After a little while, we went into the other room with Richey's grandsons and just hugged them. The boys were so devastated. We talked to the family for quite a while and then went back in to say goodbye to Richey. Carmen went up to the side of the bed and said, loudly, "Richey, its Annie and Carmen. You get better now and we'll see you tomorrow."

Rich opened his eyes, looked at Carmen and said, "Carmen, Hey!" He then closed his eyes and went back to his labored breathing sleep. Everyone was amazed. Richey had been out for most of the day. He woke and recognized Carmen. Purely miraculous.

His grandson, Adam told us at the wake that besides wishing him a happy birthday, that his words to Carmen were the last words Richey had said. I can still hear them. We brought food up to the house for the family, because that's what you do. Such a terrible loss. Rest well Richey. We miss you, and will forever remember your kindness.

Chapter 22

In September of 2008, Terry invited us to visit her in St. Louis. Being a season ticket holder for the St. Louis Rams, she wanted to take us to the opening game of the season against our New York Giants. It would be our first visit since Ken died. We looked forward to spending time with her. As we enjoyed our visit with Terry at the home she and Ken had built, there was a hurricane brewing down to the south. Hurricane Ike.

One afternoon as Ike barreled toward us, Terry and I walked along the lake near her house. The winds were very strong ahead of the storm, but it wasn't raining yet. At one end of the lake is a waterfall and from the rain the night before, it was raging over the edge. Between the howling wind and the thundering falls, I am not sure how we heard a strange bird call.

I looked up and this bird was just above our heads. I put my hand up and said, "Oh, come here" and down to my hand came Ike.

Obviously, Ike was named for the storm. Terry looked at me, "now what?" Being that she too is an animal lover, we both knew what! Ike is a beautiful Quaker parrot. Gorgeous green, blue and teal feathers. He was so relieved to be protected. We had noticed red-tailed hawks flying overhead, looking at Ike as their next meal. We brought him inside, out of the incoming storm. Ike clung to my hand as if he were afraid I'd let him go.

Terry took Carmen to a local pet store to see if there were any notices about missing birds. There were none, so Carmen bought Ike a cage, food, toys and treats. Meanwhile, I stayed at the house holding and calming this poor bird. He kept saying something to me. I couldn't make it out for the longest time. Quakers are known to be very good talkers and Ike was really trying to tell me something. Terry and Carmen got back with the cage and we got him all set up. By then it was all over for me. I was in love.

Terry got on the computer to check and see if there were any notices about lost Quaker parrots listed anywhere. She found nothing. Who knows? The way that wind was blowing with the storm, he could have come from anywhere. We left Terry's after a wonderful stay with Ike in tow. The Ram's/ Giants game had been played in spite of the hurricane. No tailgate for that game!

I must say also, that even though we were dressed in our Giant's gear, we were treated so kindly by the Ram's fans! It was amazing! We must have heard "welcome to St. Louis" fifty times! What a great time. Our Giants won, much to Terry's chagrin!

We loaded Ike and all of his new stuff in the truck and we were off. We stopped at a motel that night, and

Carmen got us a room on the ground floor. He went in and opened the window. We snuck Ike in. Management probably would have allowed us to take him in, but we weren't taking a chance. On the ride home Ike sat on Carmen's head or his shoulder and kept whispering in his ear. He was saying "give me a kiss". So that is what he was trying to tell me!

Ike quickly became one of the Wags family. He isn't too keen on the boys. He tries to bite them when they hold him. He loves Carmen and I. We now understand that he says "pretty bird", "good boy", the "give me a kiss", which is followed by a kissing noise and he laughs a lot. Any time the boys try to hold him and he tries to bite, he laughs at them. It's a riot!

Ike likes to fly around and we play "catch" with him, as he flies back and forth between us. Cj and Sam hate when I start this game, sure that Ike is going to latch on to them. Ike and I find this very amusing. He loves being held close, kissed and to be stroked under his wing. And, this doesn't surprise me, he likes Wiley. My brother used to say I have the weirdest animals. Natural enemies, supposedly, that like each other. Maybe they see that I love them all, which means they should too. Rabbits, cats, dogs and parrots, all friends. I live in Edward Hicks "The Peaceable Kingdom".

I realize that I have asked for blessings and they have been given. My life is not perfect, but no one's life is perfect. We all have our crosses to bear. It's what we do with what we have to better ourselves that counts. Nothing should be taken for granted. As impatient as I am to be further ahead, I do realize that it's going to take time.

I can't help but hurry up and wait. I'm spending too much time waiting for the "lottery" when it's right here, now. I have to stop getting overwhelmed. I have to realize that when I need help, I need to ask. If I need a break, I have to take it. I have to make myself happy and not wait for someone to do it for me. I'm wasting too much time hoping for something better. Carmen just walked by. He says this should be "Carmen is an asshole book". Ugh! Get back to work. He's having a bad day...

Chapter 23

April 20, 2009

How do I? How can I? What do I do?
Two years ago we left our home due to
horrible circumstances. My life, as it had
been, ended. Now Jim, the man that
bought our house shows up and says
he's selling it. He hasn't spoken to a
realtor yet, he wanted to speak to us
first. His wife always said it wasn't her
house. That's because it's mine still. In
my dreams I wander around there, tend
the flowers I planted, swim in my pool, I
play my drums in our basement.

So much time has passed. So much
has changed. We have accomplished so
much. Do I want to go back? I always
say I want to go home, but is that still
home? Dare I even wish it? God help
me, I don't know what to do or think. Is
this a test? How can we manage it with
the business?

I am so conflicted. We have two households now. Does CJ want to merge? He's been on his own for 2 years, he's 24 now. Does he want to come back home with us? I just don't know what to think.

Maybe it's time to move on. Close that chapter. I don't know. Money is the issue. We are living here, surviving. What should we do? I don't talk to anyone about it, can't speak of it. I am so conflicted. We could go home! That's what I keep saying I want, but do I? Really? Bills, extra bills. I want to be smart and not broke. Do we wait? Do we jump? I want to go home, but is the cabin still home? It doesn't even look like our home anymore. Maybe I need to go inside and see. Get a feel, see if it's still home.

May 2, 2009

Two years ago at around 3 am, we left our home for the last time. Now there is a chance we may get to go home again.

"You can't go home again", it's said. The couple that bought the house are splitting up. We left due to terrible circumstances and they will be too. If I could choose for them a happy marriage or, for us, our home, I'd give them their happiness. We are okay and will be. I don't wish their sadness on anyone. I'm back in bed again. This is not a good day.

Today is May 11th, 2009. It is Lola's 2nd birthday. It is the day after Mother's Day. It is also the day Princess Kitty died. She came to us in February of 1992 and was then, two and a half to three years old. Her tail had been broken in two places, probably from someone slamming it in a door. It remained crooked her whole life. It didn't bother her, didn't bother us.

Princess was beautiful. Prettiest eyes I've ever seen, green with flecks of deeper green and gold. She was a healer, always taking pain away from anyone dealing with it. Soft as a bunny.

Her fur, silky. Black and white. She purred all of the time. She was the most loving cat. Princess loved Woody so much she went into mourning for a year after he died. She learned to love Wiley, and Lola and Clark. For that matter, she either liked or tolerated all of our guests.

Princess had declined in the last year or so. Lately, she threw up more than the usual hairball and she took to howling. She would stare at a wall and just cry. She had gone deaf. Carmen and CJ took her to see our vet today and the vet found Princess had a serious heart murmur as well as lumps on her kidneys. She would never withstand treatment so she was put to sleep at 10:40 am.

Once again, I am dealing with a broken heart. My Princess Kitty is gone. I just heard her whine again, in my head, and probably will for a long time. Seventeen years we had her. Almost as long as Sammy! She was the best kitty. I'm never going to see her again in this life.

My little snuggle bunny, so soft. Oh God, I hate this!

Amazing how we can determine the life span of our beloved pets, determine when enough suffering is enough, yet not for ourselves. How different would our lives be if we knew when the end would be? Why isn't suicide, assisted suicide legal? We are too irrational to make that choice for ourselves and too rational to make it for others, except out pets who, don't have a voice in it either way. If there is a God in heaven, and I know there is, take good care of my kitty. I love her so much. And please, find us a home soon.

May 12, 2009

Carmen called Jim and told him no on the house. Our house, our Princess gone. I am so not happy, I just exist. Each day is the same. I eat and then feel huge. No sleep, no concentration. I miss normal sleep, miss my home and my kitty. Miss real happiness, miss real

fun. I miss Carmen, I miss everything.
Going to sleep, don't want to wake up.
Need a break, I just need a break...

May 13, 2009
  Beautiful day. Sunny and warm. Had
the carpets cleaned so CJ and I came
outside to sit in the sun. I love how I
can sit with my boys and not talk about
anything, or about everything. Nice. I'm
lucky that way, and blessed. They drive
me crazy but, I love them. I wish Sam
would show a bit more respect to his dad
and I and do what he's told without an
argument. He should become a lawyer!
Always an argument. Now I know how
my mom felt when she told us to do
something and we'd drag our feet. Ugh.
Did I mention that it's beautiful out?

May 19, 2009
  Why in the world am I awake??? I am
so tired and sore. Being awake doesn't
make sense to me at all. I woke at 1:28
am and it's now 2:02 and I'm still awake.

Sammy left his television on so I had to find his remote and turn it off. Then the hot flashes kicked in, yeah, along with everything else I'm dealing with "mentalpause"! Now I am light headed, hungry and awake! And thirsty! What the hell?

My stomach finally stopped hurting when I fell asleep as it was bothering me all day. I need sleep. I need a break, God help me, I need a break. We have been so busy and the next two weeks are going to be even more so, thank you God again. Just wish I could snap out of this insomnia thing. Maybe I should just stay up all night and write the next great novel and then sleep all day.

It's supposed to be 71 tomorrow, then into the mid 80's the rest of the week. Wow, and today I was shivering. I brought the plants in due to a freeze warning last night. We had to turn the heat on for the first time in a long time and, hopefully, the last for a long time! If I didn't hurt so bad, I go downstairs

and do laundry, not gonna happen.
Going to try to sleep again. God Bless
us everyone!

May 21, 2009
   I'm so tired. Night sweats again even
with the air on. Now I'm hungry again
too! Crap! This is so not right. What
am I going to do? I need to sleep, I
know I fell asleep, and slept for a little
while, but now I'm wide awake again. I'll
say my rosary again. Talking to God
helps. I keep praying to get the anger
out of Carmen. I hope it's working.
Stress is a terrible thing. Does terrible
things to your mind and body. I need a
miracle, light bill is due. Where are my
angels? Tomorrow Frank and OZ go to
their new home.   At least it will get us
out of here for a little while, if CJ is
feeling better that is. He's got a cold.

Chapter 24

Frank and Oz are two dachshunds that we rescued. We got a call from a woman who asked for our help, and as usual, we obliged. Their mom, P, had to move out of her house to an apartment that didn't allow pets so she had to give them up. We promised to take care of the dogs and to find them a good home. She also told us that she needed help moving. Not wanting to see someone get taken advantage of, we did that too.

With the help of the boys, we packed up all of P's stuff and got her in to her new apartment. She had a company that was going to come in and clean out everything that she left. They were going to charge her a fortune, so again, we took the challenge. P said she didn't want anything that she left behind because that was her old life and she was starting a new one. She told us to take whatever we thought we could use at Wags. We did.

We boxed up paintings and books and dishes and so much stuff and brought it to Wags. What we didn't use here, we donated to the Salvation Army and to the Fingerlakes SPCA in Auburn, New York. I just find it ironic that in the midst of trying to build this business and save ourselves, we are still trying to help others. As I have said before, isn't that what we are supposed to do? In helping P, and others, we are helping ourselves too.

May 22, 2009

Stupid knees, they hurt all of the time. No sleep consistently in over a week. Actually longer, but who's counting? Eight hour nights don't happen, I'm tired. Lola is with me for my nap. She is already asleep and snoring. Carmen is out mowing the lawn. If I had a million dollars, I'd take my whole family on a cruise. All of us, my parents, my siblings, and all the kids too. Just to spend time with them.

I miss them. I really miss Mary. And her girls. I want to go see them, but all we do is work. Sam has his play tonight and tomorrow night too. I have to call Mom and Dad and see if they want to go. Man, Lola is loud!

May 25, 2009

I don't know why I'm crying right now. It's beautiful outside today. The Memorial Day parade is going on. I used to go. I heard, but did not see, the Air Force jets fly over. I used to watch it from the porch of our house, could see them come in from one side of the valley and fly out the other. Flying parade to parade. Those days are gone. The house is up for sale again. The owners are getting divorced. I just solved the crying mystery.

Carmen went and saw the cabin and said he got a bad vibe. Maybe I need to see and feel it for myself. Who am I

kidding? We can't afford it anyway. We are stuck here. At least we got a new bed. I love it. I did laundry and cleaned today. We had a couple of messy guests here this weekend.

My wrist has been bothering me lately. It hurts and is swollen. I don't know why or what brought the swelling on. My handwriting is horrible some days due to the swelling. I always took pride in my handwriting.

We went and saw the play Sammy is in. It was written and directed by his friend Dan. Blows my mind, the talent there. I was so proud of Sammy's performance. He was so good. I don't think a lot of people got the whole premise of the story. I thought it was brilliant! Bridget and Nick stopped up for a beer last night. It was nice. I'm glad they are still in our lives. Some stay, others go. My family is heading to Pennsylvania to my cousin's wedding in a couple of weeks, Tom and Lisa included. Tom won't be here for Old

Home Days. No parade this year. It's just as well, we will be busy.

Last night was dreadful. I needed to talk. I needed to talk about the house, and I needed Carmen to just sit and listen to me. When I sat on his leg and started talking, he went off. He told me it's not going to happen. Buying any house now is just a pipe dream. It was horrible, but I guess I have to face the truth. I can't because it hurts so much. He kept saying to get over it. It was just awful.

It's bringing me down to look at pictures of our house on the realtor's web site and thinking about our life there. I don't know why I even look. Just going by the house hurts so much. I thought I was over it, but seeing the pictures made me so homesick. My stomach has been upset since Sunday night.

I used to trust my gut on everything but not anymore. I can't count on anything except that I'm stuck here. For how long? I don't know. Carmen won't stay at CJ's even though he asks us to. Maybe I'll go alone. I don't know. So much crap is going thru my head. I took an antacid for my stomach, didn't help. I've been sleeping late every morning because I don't sleep at night. I got up at 11am yesterday and today, Carmen came up at some point and I finally got up at 1 pm.

My body feels as if it is shutting down. Just part of the perpetual depression, I guess. It's true that you don't realize what you have until you no longer have it. I don't think I ever took for granted that we owned that wonderful house. I thanked God for it every day, but it was there every day. In that respect, I did take the house for granted. We, I, became very comfortable with the idea that no matter what, I could go back to that house and it was mine.

I feel now as if I'm waiting, hovering, suspended in a bubble of the past. I can't go back to that house. I can't go forward. It's as if time is standing still, or that I'm stuck in a place outside of what is real. I'm waiting for my life as it used to be, to start up again. I don't know why. I think I know that won't happen. This is just a really strange place that I am in right now.

I am also waiting to get back to me physically. I have never had pain like what I experience now. I could over do before and would always bounce back, and really quickly. That is not the case anymore. I don't get that second wind. It takes me longer to get back to feeling okay. I realize that I am getting older, that is inevitable, but what I didn't think would happen to me, ever, is.

I have always been one to do things myself, to take control of a situation and figure out how to work it out. I don't like spinning my wheels. I get a task and get to it. My head is so screwed up, I find myself analyzing and reanalyzing everything I do.

I have to look over a task so many times just to figure out where to start. I am overwhelmed very easily. I think because I have so much going on in my head, whereas before, I was relatively calm. I have been taken out of my comfort zone. What used to be important as a first step in finishing something, doesn't seem to be. It's like my dreams. They too have been so screwed up lately.

Dreams, when I do in fact sleep, about houses that I've never seen before or people I have never met. These people are so real and important when I'm sleeping, but I have no idea who they are when I wake up!

I feel as if I'm forgetting something or someone, as if I have already forgotten. These dreams are real, tangible and frequent. And a bit unnerving. I want to stay asleep so I can figure them out! They are, however, just dreams. Dreams with no meaning.

Grace is bringing Buck in tomorrow. She gives me hope. Grace is also a wonderful cheerleader. She makes us know that we are going in the right direction. She knows how hard it is to start a business and to be in a similar situation as we are. Grace makes me want to work harder, to work thru my pain. She makes me feel good about me. That's refreshing. God please bless and watch over Grace. Keep her safe and give her happiness always. Time to keep my mind fresh with a crossword puzzle. Lola is snoring, as usual!

Chapter 25

June 4th, 2009

Ouch, I am sun burned! I mowed the lawn today. Being ourside all day was great. The lawn looks like a golf course. We had only been at Wags a short time when the lawn mower we had at the house, died. I didn't know what we were going to do. June and Rob happened to be here when it happened.

There is no way we were going to able to get a new one and our lawn here is huge and needs to be kept short to avoid fleas and ticks. Ticks don't jump, they crawl. Longer grass makes that easy for them to do, so a short lawn is very helpful.

Without even a hesitation, June and Rob offered to help us buy a new mower. I don't know what I would do without my Angels on Earth! People come in to your life at different times for different reasons. We are put in a certain place for a certain reason at a certain time. No coincidences. I'm learning to be grateful for that, for the people and things that have come into our life since. And I take nothing for granted. Ever. I guess June and Rob didn't just happen to be here when we needed them...

A new customer, Bonnie, came in one day. That is not accurate. Bonnie doesn't "just go in" anywhere. She ARRIVED! She needed to board her Bishons, Mini and Rocky. She brought them in with a two page information sheet on the dogs and a school calendar for 2008-2009. On the calendar, she had circled, in red pen, all of the days that she would need to have the boys stay with us. The information sheet has the dogs history on it which includes how happy they are, but also that they have very special needs.

Mini has seizures about three times a month and has had gum disease which resulted in teeth being pulled. Rocky is only three but has had two back surgeries due to degenerative disks. Bonne included a feeding schedule and a thank you note for taking care of them. Rocky follows Mini everywhere. If they are apart, they cry. This would inevitably happen when they are groomed. We fixed that by taking them in the salon together.

They really depend on each other. They also love Wiley. Bonnie had a big dog before Rocky, an Akita, so Mini was all about hanging out with Wiley. Rocky, he has a very outgoing personality. Everyone is his friend. They do great at Wags.

What can I say about Bonnie? She is a very dynamic person. To start, she is beautiful. I once asked her if she had been a beauty pageant contestant, or model, or something, and she just laughed. No, she was a teacher, a principal, a school administrator, but not a beauty queen! She has amazing cheekbones, blond hair, beautiful eyes and a beautiful personality. She also has the most incredible laugh! It's a no holds barred, all out, expel the demons, clean out the cobwebs, laugh. A laugh of pure joy. I love it!

With Rocky and Mini in tow, Bonnie comes in to the shop. She and I usually end up outside, taking our conversation out with us after Mimi and Rocky are safely in their room. There is always something going on in Bonnie's life. She is a whirling dervish of activity! We got talking one day about places we love and she told me about her place on Longboat Key. Well, that just happens to be one of my favorite places too!

During our adventure time in Florida, we spent many a day on the beaches of Longboat Key. There, and on Anna Maria Island. She causally said that if we ever wanted to visit Florida, we could use her villa on Longboat. Well, that was really nice for her to say! Not being one to ever take an offer like that too seriously, as most times it's said fleetingly, I thanked her, but knew we never would.

I am meeting the most dynamic,
amazing people being here!

June 20, 2009
 I went and saw my doctor Nancy
yesterday because I have the flu. She's
kind of angry with me because it's been
a while since I last saw her. I have to go
back for a physical and all the stuff that
goes with that! Maybe she can figure out
why my legs hurt all the time and why I
am so tired all the time. Maybe different
blood tests, I don't know. She yells at
me about taking care of myself and also
listens when I feel like I can't do another
day. She helps. I love her for caring
about me.
 Sammy is at Relay for Life at the park,
it's a cancer fund raiser. He's walking for
Uncle Ted.   Carmen and I were alone at
Wags with our guests last night. It was
very quiet. Good group. I got up at two
this afternoon. I guess I needed to sleep
this flu off and just get rid of it. Maybe
shake off the last two years too. I feel

like I'm coming back. I need to come back. I cannot and will not let this black take me over. I need to get out of the black. Baby steps...

Things are just so busy I can't find time to sit and write. I haven't written in so long. So many new guests. I'm busy all the time. I have no time to think about what was. Only about what is, now. I know that I am feeling "better". I think that means that I can take each day as it comes and not expect success to happen overnight. The response to Wags has been phenomenal. We couldn't have asked for more. Thank you notes come all the time in the mail and it means everything to me.

I don't want to miss anything. I love my guests, love being surrounded by them. Yeah, it's pretty great sometimes, I must admit. Some guests are a challenge, but I don't lose. I want each of our guests to feel special when they are with me. I want to give them what Woody was not when he was boarded years ago. I think of Woody every day. We are so blessed to have Wiley.

We are blessed in many ways. I was too absorbed in my sadness to realize it. I talk to God every day, all the time. I feel like I'm being heard again. It's a really good feeling. Meeting people like Grace, she gives me such hope. The friends I have made, like Bonnie, and so many others! It's nice being treated as a friend. I like that. I didn't need anyone to make me feel less than I am. I was doing a good job of that myself. I know better. Feeling valueless is a pretty awful feeling. Being validated by someone you respect is awesome.

Chapter 26

January 2010

I still get really homesick for our house, but I realize that house isn't ours anymore. I get very tense whenever we drive by. I change my route rather than go by the house. If Carmen is driving, I close my eyes and pray when we pass. That house was such a huge part of our lives. I guess it will take a while to get over.

Maybe once we have a new place of our own or we make the shop more comfortable, more, homey, I'll feel relaxed. It's been a while since I've written. Things have been going, I was going to say smoothly, but that's not really the case. We've been working our butts off.

The grooming salon is operational, and we have a really good client base. We have been thru a couple of groomers, but I'm sure that will work its way out in time. We'll eventually find a good fit. Eric, my sister-in-law Lisa's nephew, has started with us part time. He is a cousin by marriage to my boys, and part of their core group of friends. So nice to have an extra pair of hands! Eric does anything we ask of him. He's such a great kid.

Eric and CJ added new rooms to the middle of the building where the salon used to be located. Since we now have use of the whole building, Carmen moved the salon to the opposite side from the motel. The salon is beautiful. Great colors, really bright. I love it. It will make a really good work space for the right person.

We did Sammy's senior pictures last night. He needed them done for the yearbook. I remember when we had CJ's done professionally. The photos were beautiful, but they came at a cost. I just couldn't afford that now. The shots we took came out great and we didn't have to spend a million dollars. I'm really happy with them!

I was going to start this with: Everyone feels that they have a special reason to be here. If we don't feel that way, what is the point? The truth is, we all really do have a reason. Why the "bad" guys? What is their purpose? The Bible tells us we blew it with Eden. Eve never should have taken that apple!   We can't all be great. If we were, we'd have nothing to measure up against. Thing is, the ones that think they are so great, usually aren't. The ones that don't, usually are. Funny that. I think I'm pretty happy. I think we are doing a good thing with our business.

I know, without a doubt, I absolutely adore my dogs. They bring so much joy to me. Clark is definitely my boy. He is with me 90 percent of my day. He waits for me in bed while I shower and then snuggles up with me for our time before bed. Lola is with Carmen during this time, but sleeps on me if they sleep with us at night.

Wiley sleeps downstairs so he can keep an eye on things. He lets us know if someone needs us by barking. That includes keeping tabs on the sixteen puppies we adopted last Friday. Our vet was here today doing all of their work-ups to get them ready to go home. Now to find them homes!

So much has been going on lately. I have been thinking of book names for this story. "From Wags to Riches", maybe. "A New Leash on Life"? Not really one hundred percent sure. I kind of like "Annie Wags", sigh, but I don't know.

It's June. I've got my two puppies in bed with me. I want Lola to stop her bath as its nap time. I take a lot of naps, still. I think of my three dogs, Clark is the most attached to me. His litter was born the year after Lola's. June and Rob have their parents, Coco and Bear.

After we got Lola, we had many people inquire as to where we got her. Carmen asked June if Coco could have another litter, she could, so, June bred her. We wanted a male and customers wanted pups too. That is how we got Clark. He was the only tri-color in the litter. He is white, grey and fawn. Lola is mostly fawn in color.

Shortly after Clark's litter was born, June and Rob had to go out of town, so we brought Coco and her pups to Wags. It was a down day for me, so CJ and Sammy brought Clark up into bed with me. He was two weeks old. He got so close to me with his puppy breath and softness. It felt wonderful.

Clark's baby eyes looked at me the way Woody's did when he passed away. Straight into to my heart. Are these tears of joy for Clark or of sadness for my Woody? Both, I guess.

I will never forget Woody. Clark's middle name is Woody. Clark W. Like the dad in "National Lampoon's Family

Vacation". My dogs heal me. They are the best. They have helped me more than any medicine ever could. They know when I'm having a difficult day and snuggle a bit closer. I can look into their beautiful brown eyes and see how much they love me. I don't think I would have come this far without them. They own my heart. I think I own a bit of theirs as well.

It's beautiful outside today. In the eighties. It rained most of yesterday, though I slept through it. We need the rain. We are supposed to get thunderstorms tonight. I love that. The very best thing about a metal roof is the sound of the rain on it. Even when it's pouring, the rain on the metal makes a rhythmic, relaxing sound.

We have all of our customers fill out a profile for their pet when they come to stay, and some of our guests are afraid of storms. The rain on the metal roof is very calming. The thickness of the walls seems to absorb some of the thunder.

Very rarely do we have to do any more than turn up the volume of the TV or the radio in the main room to drown out that noise. For the most part, storms really don't bother even our most skittish guests. They are busy here. Maybe too busy to notice a storm.

Chapter 27

January 20, 2011

My dream this morning was so real. I was in my house. I had my arms and hands on the island counter. I could feel the wood of its butcher block top. I was holding it, crying because I was so happy to be home. I asked someone, I think it was my brother in law Rob, if it was real. Over and over I asked. He finally said "ask Carmen". That's when I heard footsteps coming up the stairs.

I was sort of awake. The footsteps I heard were CJ's, coming to check on me. I wasn't home. Not in my house. But here. At Wags. Again. Still. My heart is breaking.

I feel I've lost my connection with Carmen. We co-exist. Platonic. This isn't supposed to be. It's just not. Sam got some boxes out and I unpacked them yesterday looking for my bake ware. I tried to see if there was still the house smell in there. Foolish thoughts.

This is my reality now. I am so tired. I work my ass off when I'm not sleeping. That is all we do, work and sleep. I was given this life as a gift. I used to be sure of what I would tell God when I got to Heaven. I'd tell Him I didn't waste the gift, but really enjoyed it and had a blast. We had such a good life in the cabin, but it was so short lived.

CJ had the best of our former life. Sammy got cheated a bit. I have so many regrets. I'm sorry we couldn't have a party for your graduation, Sammy. Things were so tight, and we didn't have a home to host it in. We didn't have the time to plan because we are so busy working, and all of our guests. I should have appreciated what we had more when we had it. This is a really hard lesson to learn.

Okay, shake it off. No one can make your happiness for you. Trust no one to make you happy or you will be

disappointed. The romantic fantasy fades and reality sets in only to bite you in the ass. There, in the ass, because that's where your brain is sometimes. Think with your head not with your heart. Don't let your emotions rule you. No one cares about you. Everyone just cares about themselves. Only the strong survive. I don't feel strong.

I have some really great memories. They cannot be removed. Woody helping me pull weeds in front of the rock wall. Picking daffodils with Morgan for her mom. The smell of lilacs coming in my bedroom window on a cool spring breeze. Laying on the grass and watching the clouds with my boys. Playing in the yard with Woody. That is where I want to be. I just want to go home. I don't know where that is anymore.

I am physically sick because of how sad I am. I am supposed to keep it together for my boys. I have no one to talk to. I miss my brother and sisters. I have missed so much these past four years. So much. My nieces, Ducky and Lauren, I miss my silly girls. I wish you were still little and I could try again. I'd do better, I swear. But I can't go back. I am afraid to go forward because I don't trust the future.

This is the wrong plan. I miss stepped somewhere and was taken down the wrong road. I can hear my heart breaking. I wish it would stop. I hear life going on around me, without me, and that's okay. I don't want to play anymore anyway. I am so done with this. I can't do it anymore. I am so tired, so drained, so weak and no one to talk to.

I have disconnected. I want to crawl under my bed right now, maybe I will. I want to go home. I don't know where that is. Used to be in Carmen's arms, but not anymore. We are on opposite sides of the universe now, with no connection except anger. I don't want to try and work on it anymore because I just keep getting my heart broken. We don't make each other laugh anymore. It's all work, work and more work. No us time anymore. That dream really set me back. I hate my dreams.

Chapter 28

Summer, 2011

Midwinter break, spring break, Easter, Memorial Day. Any and all Holidays are absolutely crazy now. I have no time to feel sorry for myself. We have too much to do. Bad days seem to become less frequent because I am working so hard. The boys have things to do, like live their lives, so there are nights that it's just me for the walk. I don't mind.

I like the quiet time with my guests. They really help. I think this is my therapy, being with my kids. Not my boys, my furry guests. I like walking the dogs by myself because I can take my time and enjoy each one. They all have such different personalities, just like people.

Major came in with his dad, Bob, one day. Major is a huge black lab. Bob told us that Major likes to hang out and will nap in his crate most of the day. Very low key. We gave him a nice room with a bed and set his crate up in there for him to use. Nope, that wasn't going to work. He barked his dissatisfaction very soon after we closed his door.

Barking, grumbling, and growling. Major was being a grumpy old man! Okay, we'll try something different. We opened his door and disassembled his crate. We took the disassembled crate back out of his room and reassembled it in the living room. I barely had enough time to put his bed and his teddy bear back in there, than he tried to get past me and into the crate!

During one stay, I thought I'd try putting Major's crate in front of the open door to a room so he'd still have the room to use. Nope, that wouldn't do. More grumbling and barking. Major had to have his crate, his den, in the middle of the room where all of the action was. He had to be the center of the Wags universe. We were his wait staff and we were here to serve his every need!

Major was our first guest to get a visitor. We quickly learned that that was a bad idea. One of Bob's neighbors stopped in to see how Major was doing. I didn't think it would be a problem. Um, wrong. When our guests are vacationing with us and you bring a visitor in, not only does the visitee get all worked up, but every other guest does as well.

The dogs think the visit is for them or that it's time to go home. The disappointment they feel is very obvious on their face. Major barked his displeasure with the whole visitor idea loudly. He settled down after a bit, and a cookie, but I felt bad for him. We won't do that again! No more two legged visitors at Wags again!

Major came and stayed often and became one of our extended family. I found this to be happening pretty frequently with returning guests, come to think of it. But he definitely was special. If Major wanted a drink and his bowl was empty, he would pick it up and "prison cup" it along the sides of his crate. The boys gave this practice its name after old movies where prisoners in jail would rake their cups across the jail cell bars. Major would pick the bowl up, walk over to his crate, and run it down the sides of his crate! He got his point across!

He would "prison cup" when he thought it was time to eat too. It didn't matter if it wasn't time yet. Major wouldn't eat his dinner until after he was told to sit and wait, which he did. He wouldn't touch it, however, until you snapped your fingers to let him know it was okay to eat! Major was on his own clock and we were to serve him when he wanted, not when it was time. He also liked to check out what everyone else was having to eat. He'd follow us around during meal times, sniffing all the while, just checking, and grumbling, waiting for a morsel, or better yet, a treat, to be dropped.

Bob, Major's dad, would call every now and then to see how his boy was fairing, but he told us he never worried about

Major. We get that complement a lot.
We have been told repeatedly that
parents don't worry when their kids are
with us. A complement like that is really
nice.

If you spend a few minutes with us you
will see how we are with our guests.
They are a part of our family. Loving
them makes it very hard when it's time
to say goodbye. Unfortunately, having
to say goodbye happens, and the more
guests we get, the more times it will
happen.

Such was the case with Major. Bob
stopped in a few days prior to Major's
last stay. That is not unusual. People
stop in all the time to say hi or drop
something, like cookies, off. This wasn't
one of those visits. He had to tell us
Major was failing.

Bob asked if we would still take Major
as he had to go out of town. Bob knew
that he probably wouldn't be taking
Major back home. He knew how we felt
about Major and more importantly, how

Major felt about us. He didn't want to leave him with anyone else, just in case.

Of course we would take him! We then made a plan of action. Major's esophagus was slowly closing and it would come to a point where he would not be able to breathe. Reminded me of Woody. Nothing could be done because of his age. It was just a matter of time. Major had had a good, long life and now it was all about quality over quantity.

We were instructed that if Major went down, we were to call Bob's son. Major was his dog growing up, but ended up with Bob when his son moved on. Bob wanted to make sure his son was there for Major in the end. Their vet was also notified and would be ready when Major was.

On an April evening, we had finished doing the dinner feeding. Major was going door to door, as usual, checking on all of the other guest's menus. He was sneaking a pat on the head, nosing hands as we tried to feed everyone. You couldn't bend over for anything without getting a face full of that huge muzzle. He was very interested and interacting, even more than usual. After dinner, everyone settled in for a quiet evening.

At about 8 pm, we started doing a walk and Major was kind of hanging out, observing everyone and everything. We got done with the walk and as usual Major was the last one to go out. He got his leash on and we started out the door. Major got about two steps out when he collapsed. Carmen, CJ, Eric and I were by his side immediately. I cradled his head in my hands and just cried. It was his time to pass. This wonderful, beautiful baby was leaving us. He was struggling for each breath. Eric was by my side and we talked to him and told him how great he was.

Carmen had sprung into action, first calling the vet, then Bob's son. CJ went inside and got a blanket. I kept telling Major to hang in there, and not thinking, to not go. I couldn't help it. I know I shouldn't, but I cried, and hugged him, and loved him, and cried some more. I knew for him, I had to stop. I had to be strong. I had to tell him it was okay. I couldn't ask him to fight anymore. It wasn't fair for me to ask that. I soothed him, and Eric and I held him until CJ and Carmen could get him in the car.

The three of them picked Major up. He was struggling for breath. They got him in the car. I was able to say goodbye and to tell him how much he was loved by us and by his family. I told Major he was a great friend, a strong protector, a beautiful boy, and a great dog. I just sobbed as Carmen and CJ drove off.

Eric stayed with me and came and gave me a big hug and he was crying too. We waited together for Carmen and CJ to get back. I couldn't sit still so I started to clean. It's what I do when I'm upset or stressed. After what seemed like hours, my men came back.

As he laughed and cried, CJ told us about Major's last ride. On the way to the vet's office, CJ held Major in the backseat. He cried and rubbed Major's side as he soothed him. Major tried to roll on his back, struggling as he did. As he fought for breath, he pushed to get over on to his back. CJ thought he was trying to situate himself so he could breathe better. No. Not that. He wanted his belly rubbed! CJ obliged, and rubbed his belly all the way to the vet's office!

Bob's son met Carmen and CJ at the vet's office. He got to say goodbye to his old friend. Two days later, without ever knowing our Major, a customer sent us a picture of a grave marker they had seen in a pet cemetery while interring their pet. The stone said, "Major. Born a dog, died a gentleman". Perfect.

Chapter 29

Grace brings Buck by to get his groom or for a stay. She really gives me hope and brightens my day. I feel really fortunate to have her in my life. Grace brought her mother with her one day and I went out to meet her. I told her she had a wonderful daughter. Her reply, "I know". Grace's mom is a little, petite lady. She is so cute! Grace favors her. Both are spit fires, that's for sure!

Grace and her mom left Buck to get his groom and went to do their errands. The two spent at least part of everyday together. The errands today included getting us a pie from a local shop. It was lunch for us and delicious! Treats like that make my day. Small kindnesses.

Let me explain what a small kindness means to me. Small kindnesses are something you do without really giving it much thought. The gesture usually ends up being a very big deal to the person on the receiving end of it. The giver usually has no idea how much this small act may impact the receiver, in that it could be a life changer or a life saver. One day, when the giver stands in front of God, He will ask, "Do you remember when you did this small kindness?"

I have found that when the small kindness is brought to the attention of the giver, myself included, that usually, it didn't seem like that big of a deal. When you are on the receiving end of the kindness, nothing could be further from the truth. I bet Grace still has no idea how much that pie meant to me, to us. She has become someone that I really admire.

When Grace and her husband were starting their business, they struggled as we are now. Not to the same extent, but there are similarities. She is humble enough to share her stories with me. The stories give me hope. She makes me want to work harder, and to be better. I do so appreciate that! She has become a perfect ally not to mention our biggest cheerleader.

We have had so many guests since we opened and with each one, we learn something. I am dealing with losing the house so much better now. I know it's because we are so busy. I still can't look at the house when we go by. I still have issues with my anger over my loss, but it is getting better.

We have seen a few of our old gang. Some are responsive, some, not so much, but it's okay. People handle situations differently. I have come to be thankful for the times we had. I have let go of my anger. It held me back. I also realize, times change. I need to flow with that change. It's okay. Different, but okay.

Mom and Dad were in the other day and I was in the living room playing with a few of our guests. Mom peeked over the gate and said "you are in your glory, aren't you?!" Yup, guess I am. It is

what I always wanted. I never had a
dog growing up, with the exception of an
occasional stray. Now, I have every age,
breed and size I could ever need.

Our client list grows every day. We
mark the boxes of folders we buy with
the date we use the first one. We run
out a lot. Most people that stop have
been very positive, in fact, I can't think
of any one that was otherwise. So many
are coming in time after time. That is a
huge compliment.

The call came in one day from a lady
that said she needed to board her dogs.
She has three but one of them, Mikey,
isn't doing so well. Another living on
borrowed time.   She doesn't want to
leave Mikey at the vet to die alone.
She'd like to bring Mikey in with his
siblings so he can spend what time he
has left with them. "Would we be willing
and able to do that?" "Absolutely. All I
need is instructions and we'll make it
happen." Mikey came in with his
brothers and we set them up in a room

together. I didn't want him to try and jump so we have no furniture in the room, just their beds.

Mikey is blind, incontinent, and very old. He's also really cute with an amazing personality. His mom and dad said their goodbyes, just in case, gave us instructions on what to do when the time came, and left to go out of town. The three dogs settled in very well. The two younger dogs we took out separately from Mikey as they walked quickly and needed a longer walk.

Mikey, I took out, as he is pretty slow. As it was warm outside, we took our time on walks. We wouldn't go far, but stayed outside a bit longer as he seemed to enjoy it. During the day when it was quiet, Mikey would just sit on the deck up front and relax. He liked sitting with a breeze on him, and with the door right there, he got it. Plus, any time someone walked by, he'd get a pat on the head.

One evening, Mikey was making a fuss in his room. I thought he needed to go to the bathroom. I went and got him, and even though it was pouring outside, I grabbed an umbrella and out we went. Mikey just wanted to lay in the wet grass. I knelt down on the ground next to him.

  With umbrella in hand, I sat with him, in the rain. The air was so fresh and clean. The ground was saturated. You could smell the brown of the earth. It was wonderful.   He thoroughly enjoyed being in the rain. So did I. It was so peaceful. Now I understand why he wanted to go out. I petted his wet face and we enjoyed the quiet rain together.

  When he had had enough, Mikey got up and I helped him inside. I got a warm towel out of the dryer and toweled him off. He was exuberant. So happy. There is nothing like a warm towel when you are cold and wet from the rain!

  Mikey and I got into the habit of sitting on the deck most of the day. He liked socialization, and the other guest would give him a sniff when they passed, and go on their way. Dogs are so much better about their elders than people are. Dogs are more courteous, kinder and, respectful. Even dogs that don't necessarily like other dogs, will respect an older dog.

After a day where Mikey ate little and just seemed worn out, he sat on the deck while we did the evening walk. We had a full house, which at the time was about twelve rooms. Each guest came and gave him a sniff when they went out and, again, when they came back in. He loved it. His tail never stopped. That night, we put him in his bed with his siblings beside him, and said goodnight. It was a very quiet night.

The next morning, I went in Mikey's room to get him for his walk. He laid at peace, all cozy in his bed, with his brothers next to him. He had passed away in the night. I had spoken to his vet before his stay for instructions. I was told what to look for, and what to expect. I was told Mikey would probably have seizures, convulse, vomit, defecate or suffer before passing.

None of this happened. He got a kiss goodnight, went to bed with brothers that he loved, and went to sleep. It was perfect. And it was heartbreaking. It was also absolutely silent for the morning walk. So weird. No one barked to go out, or to eat. Just silent. They knew. They respected.

We gave Mikey's brothers time to say goodbye in their way. Carmen snipped a bit of his hair for us to have and for his mom, and we wrapped Mikey up in a blanket, and took him to be cremated as per his mom's wishes. We gently placed Mikey in the back of the truck with his face uncovered for the ride. Dogs love to ride with the wind in their face.

Mikey had the wind in his face one last time. Blessed is he who has been loved by a dog. I am so grateful to his family for trusting us with Mikey. I feel that we were honored to share his last days. His brothers got lots of extra attention, as they were mourning the loss of their brother.

Chapter 30

We have been given more furniture along the way. Items people didn't want to throw away. We have also been getting blankets, sheets, and towels. We had received so many that we donated the overflow to the Fingerlakes SPCA in Auburn, New York. Carmen and I took a bunch of stuff there for the animals, and the volunteers couldn't be happier. We also visited the animals that were there. It is so sad how many animals are there because they are lost or unwanted, or unable to be cared for.

Carmen and I knew that we weren't going to bring anyone home. We just wanted them to see a friendly face. Seeing these babies in cages was pure torture for us both. We want to bring every one of them, dogs, cats, rabbits, all of them home, well, back to Wags. We didn't, but we promised to keep bringing stuff and we have.

Some of our clients found out about our donations to the SPCA, and have dropped off more blankets and towels and pet food. We also take our beverage cans there so the volunteers can redeem the deposit for cash. Every little bit helps. When we opened the new salon, we took some of our unneeded, gently used grooming tools to them as well.

Here we are, again, living at Wags and helping these dogs. I hadn't really thought about that until I wrote it down. Karma works. We have been making the SPCA runs, and in return, we are meeting the most incredible people and dogs! And things aren't so black anymore. I enjoy what I'm doing so much! We knew that there was a need for out kind of service, but, wow, I never imagined to this extent! No coincidences.

August, 2011
Grace called. Her mom passed away. Grace is devastated. And, she has a

problem. Her mom has a dog, a dachshund, named Mandy. Grace doesn't know what to do with her. I told her I'd take her until they can figure things out. Her mother's death came very suddenly and unexpectedly. Things for Grace are very chaotic right now. We wanted to help anyway we could.

In came Mandy. Talk about a prima donna!!! She came in here like she owns the place. We told Grace that Mandy can stay with us at Wags, for as long as she needed her to. A few days later Grace told us that her mom wanted to be buried with Mandy. Um, Mandy is still alive. We love her. We made some calls, but decided to give Grace some time to figure out what she wanted to do.

Kiddingly, CJ suggested that we go find some road kill, cremate it and give the ashes to Grace to be buried with her mom. Mandy wasn't going anywhere. Ok, but then what happens when Grace's family finds out it's not Mandy, but road kill??? Oh, that would be bad. We'd never do that anyway. It was only suggested to lighten the mood. I'm sure Grace's family will figure it out.

A little bit goes by and Grace calls back. We are told that there was a misunderstanding. Her mom would never want Mandy put down so she could be buried with her! Whew, that's better. No road kill hunt then. Mandy would be staying with us until we could give her a proper home or, if not, she can stay with us the rest of her days. Crisis avoided. Thank you God!

(Just an afterthought: Although we try and do whatever we are asked in regards to our guests, we do understand that they are not ours. The owner's wishes always come first. We would have never given Grace road kill ashes. It was said in jest, as I said, to lighten the somber mood we were experiencing due to Graces' mother's passing. There is absolutely no disrespect intended. Grace knows this, and understands our feelings

toward Mandy, her mother and herself.
Thank you.)

Mandy is either 11 or 12 years old. She certainly doesn't act her age. She's going to be around a while! Grace gave us a check for anything that Mandy may need, so the first thing we did was get her to her vet. She had a thorough exam and all of her vaccinations updated. We then gave Mandy a lovely spa day, including bath, ears and nails. She looked and felt lovely! She has now made herself right at home.

After staying with us awhile, Carmen had an idea. He'd call one of our customers, Bob, and his wife, Betty. Their dachshund, Charlie, had passed away recently. Maybe they are ready for a new friend. It's worth a shot. Carmen first called Grace with the idea of giving Mandy a new home. That would be fine with her. Then Carmen called Bob.

Bob was kind of on the fence about getting another dog, but said he and Betty would come meet her. Remember

I said that you can't just "go look" at a dog?. Mandy sauntered out of the living room to greet them. It wasn't long before she was nestled in the crook of Betty's arm just as happy as could be. Mandy had been a bit standoffish toward some people, but she took right to Betty and Bob. Mandy has a new home.

Carmen called Grace and let her know that Mandy, Bob and Betty were a perfect fit. Grace was grateful that we had waited on doing anything about Mandy until she could absorb some of her loss. Losing her mom was really hard, she didn't need to lose Mandy too. Now Mandy would be starting a new life with Bob and Betty. It couldn't have worked out better. Carmen also told her about the road kill replacement plan. That gave Grace a laugh!

Not long after Mandy went home with them, Bob started not feeling well. He was diagnosed with Parkinson's disease and ended up in a rehab facility. What got him back home was Mandy. What kept Betty going in Bob's absence was Mandy. We are exactly where we are supposed to be at any given moment. No coincidence. Grace found us for a reason. Mandy was sent to us to help Bob and Betty. They needed each other.

We still get to see Mandy as Bob and Betty travel out of town to see their grandkids. She reverts back to feeling as she owns the place! Mandy and Buck have come in to stay at the same time. They always remember each other and it is a wonderful reunion.

About a month after her mother died, Grace came in to drop off Buck for a visit. She casually told Carmen and I that her mother's house was being cleaned and readied for sale. "Why don't you stop by and look at it". We have known Grace long enough to know that she cares about us. She knows how we got here, and about our house situation. Okay, it's a quiet day, we'll go.

The house is nestled in a quiet, park-like neighborhood. It is a cute and cozy

home. The yard is huge and beautiful.
It's close to Wags and everything we
could need. There are men at the house
now, sanding and refinishing the wood
floors. We peeked in. It's adorable. I
love the house, we can't afford it, but it's
a great house

We are still building Wags. We are
doing well, but we are growing and
growth costs money. We are rebuilding
our credit. It's going to take a while to
be able to get a mortgage. It's a nice
thought. Who knows? Maybe it won't
sell for a while and if we save up enough
for a down payment, maybe someone
will work with us. Is that hope I feel?
Sept. 8, 2011

We went to brunch today with Grace.
We were supposed to be going to lunch,
but it was early, and Grace said
breakfast was really good at a little place
in Skaneateles. Our meal was good, and
it was nice to see Grace again. She
seemed better. I know she misses her
mom.

Grace spent a part of everyday with her mom, taking her shopping or for a drive. They just liked being together. She checked on her mother constantly and was ever the doting, attentive daughter. If Grace called her mother and there was no answer, she would run to her house and find out why. They had a great relationship, and a deep fondness for each other. Grace seemed a little lost without her.

Grace informed us that she is not showing her mother's house to anyone else. She showed it to us and her mom's home is to be our home. She is not going to list it with a realtor. I am psyched. I don't want to be excited because I'm afraid, but she told me not to worry, it is ours. Looking forward to something. That hasn't happened in a long time. I like this hope that I'm feeling again!

We will be attending Todd's Fund on Saturday. Todd's Fund is a benefit honoring a young man from Skaneateles, who was killed on 9/11 in the North Tower of the World Trade Center where he worked. Our friend Jill asked us to donate a gift certificate for the silent auction they hold. She helps showcase the live part of the auction.

We have donated a gift certificate to Todd's Fund for the last two years, as all funds go to helping local children and families in need. This will be Carmen and my first time attending. There will be a dinner and dancing along with the auction. We are going with Jill, her husband John, and Bridget and Nick. It will be fun! Maybe this is the winds of change. Today is a good day!

We did indeed go to the Todd's Fund Benefit on September 10th. It was a blast! Probably the most fun I've had since the house. Dinner was wonderful. There was music, and dancing, and the auction went really well. It was great to get dressed up and not worry about work. It was even better being with friends and laughing again.

As we were having dinner, Todd's family and friends got up and spoke about Todd. There was a moment of silence for all of those lost. I thought about how many people were doing the same thing we were right then, honoring their loved ones. Candles were lit, heads bowed in prayer, silence surrounded us in reverence for the dead. Such a profound loss.

Chapter 31

September 17, 2011

Sammy is 20. He said he wouldn't grow up, well, get big, and yet, he is. My baby has grown up. Where did the time go? When did this happen? I had to get away today, so I took a drive. I didn't want to come back. I'm tired of everyone telling me what I am supposed to do, or ought to be doing. I am sick of hearing, "ya know what I'd do?"! Well, I didn't ask your opinion and it's none of my business what you think! I am so tired and so sore. My legs are killing me. So, what's the real problem?

September 22, 2011

I am fifty years old. Really? Fifty. 50! I am 50. My 50 year old ass just got breakfast in bed brought to me by CJ, my 26, soon to be 27, year old son. Fifty. Image that. (ugh!) Imagine that. See, so old I forgot how to spell.

Carmen, Terry, Sammy and I went to the Meadowlands on Sunday for a New York Football Giants, Monday night game against the Rams. We had dinner at the "Al Di La" restaurant near the stadium Sunday night. It was wonderful. We tried to get a bus into the city, but the busses were packed due to the Jets game being played that afternoon. We did go in to the city on Monday. Went to Ground Zero, around the new construction, and walked around St. Paul's. We visited Battery Park and Times Square.

The city is beautiful on a sunny day. I would really love to go back and spend a week there just looking at everything. I gave Mickey Mouse a High five in Times Square. Wish I had a picture of that! So much going on. It's so alive in the City. Like a bee hive with everyone buzzing about, going here and there.

I don't know that I'd like to work there, but to just "be" there. I'd want to do the city at my own leisure. Take my time to take everything in. Spend the night in the city. See Central Park, the Dakota, Central Park West and Brooklyn, the Bronx and Tribecca. Rockefeller Center and Plaza. Got to an Irish Pub. Go back to Ground Zero again now that I know what I'm looking at, and for.

My heart aches for all of those people lost on 9/11, and their survivors. A lot of those killed were living their dream. They died in a nightmare. I hope God spared them fear and dismay. I hope He took them before they really knew what was happening.

And the perpetrators. They are the misguided, believing that God could be hateful and vengeful. They can't know God if that's what they believe of Him. Misled and misguided by hate mongers. They don't know a God of love and kindness.

The murderers of 9/11 were taught an ugly hate and it finally consumed them. People can be cruel and vicious, but I think that much hate can only be taught.

Can people really be born with that much hate and evil in their soul? Maybe so, probably so? I wish it weren't so. Such a frightening thought.

It's been a long time since I was in New York City last. Not since our visits with Aunt Anne. It is such an amazing city. I love the buildings, the noise the hustle and bustle. Carmen, not so much. I think it was too much for him. Sammy came with us and was enjoying it as much as I was. I'd love to go again with him. Terry enjoyed it too. It was a great day.

The Giants played the Rams on Monday night and, again, the Giants won. Great game. Always is when you are right there. Before the game, we donned our jerseys, Carmen, Sam and I in Giants gear. Terry in her Rams blue and gold. A woman, seeing Terry's jersey, came up and asked her if she wanted to be on a new TV show called "The Chew". She said they were going to be filming a segment for the show's debut.

Chef Michael Symon would be doing a competition involving hamburgers, St. Louis style and New York City style. Terry participated, of course. Sam and I were in the background crowd. It was fun! A contestant representing each fan base, Terry being one, tasted each burger and picked the winner. Unlike the football match-up, I believe the burger from St. Louis won.

Carmen drove us home after the game. We got in at about four in the morning and I was up again and working by eight. Wednesday, Terry went back home. She had stayed with us at Wags this visit. Terry is the kind of person that doesn't mind where she is as long as she's with the ones she loves. Carmen and I love her for that. We set up a little guest nook for her, and it worked out well. I am so sore today. I know I over did it, but what are the alternatives. Sit around all day and become immobile? No. I just, I don't know.

Thank God for my puppies. They help me recover. Clark is upside-down and being cute. Lola is asleep on my foot. She loves me. He adores me. Anything I do to Clark, he loves. Anything I ask him to do, he does. He is so devoted and just wants to be near me. I love it. He is so adorable. I don't want Lola to think I don't love her as much, because I do. It's just that he is so much more affectionate. I can't imagine my life without Lola and Clark in it. I could never survive my life without my dogs.

Chapter 32

September 27, 2011

Bonnie came for a visit last night, after hours. She's been going through a tough time and we have a friend that we knew could guide her in the right direction. He got Bonnie through her difficulties and back on top of her world. We remained a constant for her, being there whenever she needed us.

Her daughter, Kelly, was going to be visiting colleges, so we took Bonnie's dogs for her whenever she went. Mini passed away during this rough time, and Rocky was so depressed. Bonnie called to talk about Rocky one day, and asked what she could do for him. I told her to bring Rocky here for the day.

When two dogs have been together as long as Mini and Rocky had, it is often devastating for the survivor. Just like people, they need to be surrounded by their friends while grieving. Bonnie brought Rocky in for daycare. We had Wiley waiting at the door for him. As he neared the door, Rocky had his head down, tail down, really looking sad. When he came in the door, there was Wiley. Rocky's head came up, tail up and wagging, he was amongst friends. They both went to the gate and waited to be let into the living room where they continued their conversation. It was as if Rocky was telling Wiley of Mini's passing.

The rest of the day Rocky spent with Wiley, Lola, and Clark. Just being with his friends made all the difference in the world to him. Rocky went home happy. Bonnie was relieved as she was worried about him.

We have done daycare many times for guests that have lost a loved one, human or animal. It works every time. We went and adopted a few more shihtzus and Kelly fell for one in particular, Dewey. He's adorable. We introduced Dewey to Rocky and they took to each other right away. Rocky and Dewey are so good together. Now Rocky is the big brother and he loves his role. It's great when you can place a dog like that. It is so rewarding.

So anyway, Bonnie came to Wags last night, we had pizza and a glass of wine. It was nice. I love our conversations. Bonnie and I got talking about Longboat Key again. It always goes back to Longboat! I love it there. Would love to move back if not for the boys, my parents, Wags. Carmen had his laptop out and found Bonnie's villa on a map. She asked if we would like to go to Longboat and stay at the villa.

Bonnie had asked us this question before, soon after we met. I didn't think that she really meant it. Knowing Bonnie as I do now, I know she does. Absolutely! My nephew, Tommy is getting married on October first, we can leave the next day. Is this for real??? As a gift to Carmen and I for helping her, Bonnie booked our flights. I am in total shock and disbelief. So, we are leaving,

really, October second. I'm floored!!!
And excited.

Tommy and Jessica's wedding was
beautiful. They are both so stinking
cute. Christopher was the best man. CJ,
Eric and a friend of theirs, Mikey were
the ushers. They looked so handsome!
When did this happen that they all grew
up? Young, good men, all of them. I am
so proud of them. Lisa and I knew this
would happen. We talked about it when
they were little, how they would grow up
together, be best friends and end up in
each other's wedding. It was inevitable.

Tommy is the first of my parent's
grandkids to be married. It just doesn't
seem possible. They will always be little
to me even if they tower over me!
Carmen had lost his wedding ring a long
time ago and we had gotten him a new
one, but it hadn't been blessed. The
wonderful priest that celebrated the
wedding mass came to the reception.
There, Carmen asked Father Lang to
bless our rings which he did. It was

lovely. Thirty-one years together, thirty of those married. I hope Tommy and Jess have a long and blessed life together.

Carmen and I didn't go to bed after the reception. We went back and packed and waited to go to the airport. The adrenaline was keeping us up. It was our Honeymoon. We never had one as we eloped, so this would be it. Our flight was at 6 am. We landed in Sarasota at 10:50 am. Paradise. Yes, this is the perfect place to write. Thank you Bonnie!

After a good nap, we got up and ordered pizza. It was wonderful. Everything on our own time. No schedule. Carmen and I had a nice relaxed evening and we got a good night's sleep. There is an amazing breeze here today. Yesterday afternoon a cold front blew through and after being at the beach all day with temps in the upper 70s, today is a bit of a shock. As a northerner like myself, it is perfect.

Cool and breezy. Just exactly the way that I feel.

Every few seconds there is a splashing from the mullet jumping in Sarasota Bay outside of the lanai. They look like stones skipping across the water leaving barely a ripple in their wake. Out farther in the bay, dolphins. It looks like at least two. Bobbing up and out of the calm water. No boats out there to dodge today.

At low tide yesterday, there were people out in the bay on a sand bar digging something, oysters maybe. They had lots of company with all of the cranes, heron and egrets. It is so beautiful here. Sarasota Bay in the backyard and across the street, the Gulf of Mexico.

We have been traveling around the island revisiting places from our adventure years here. Carmen got a hold of his friend Bert and his wife Kelly and we have been going to dinner and just spending time together. We got a hold of my friend Melanie too. It's so nice to be with our Florida friends again! We have found new restaurants and bars on Anna Maria Island. Some of our favorites have long gone and there are many new ones in their place.

The island still feels the same as it did twenty years ago. Just newer in places. One special place we found is a wonderful coffee shop that also sell lots of handmade items and refurbished old items. I love it and want everything they sell. It's so cozy and their coffee and desserts are delicious.

Carmen and I head to the beach every day to just unwind and to get rid of some of the grime from the last couple of years. A beach baptism, a soul cleansing. I feel renewed. I feel like I'm getting me back. I am seeing a lot more of the man I fell in love with all of those years ago as well. From all that we have been through, and all that is still to come, we are still us. Different, more resilient, but completely and utterly, us.

We came back home, refreshed and ready to go on. Everything went smoothly in our absence. CJ and Sammy did really well holding down the fort. I looked forward to going back to work. In the truck on the way back from the airport, CJ told us that Ike died. I am crushed. It happened hours before we got home. Sammy said it looked like he fell asleep on his perch, then told me it was because he missed me. Brat. I can't believe it. No more "give me a kiss".

Grace's husband called and gave Carmen a price for his mother-in-law's house and the terms. We discussed the price and decided we just can't do it now. Carmen called Grace back and thanked her for considering us, but that right now, we just can't. I wanted to have Ike at the house when we got it, he would have loved the sunroom.

No Ike, no sunroom, just Wags. And that is enough. I am so grateful for what we do have. I can't think about what might have been. I would have loved my

life there, but, it's okay. We'll get there.
Put yourself back at Longboat...

It's cold and rainy like a mid-October
day should be. I'm going to take a nap
as this weather really shuts me down.
Lola is next to me, tight against my side
keeping my right hip warm. Clark, he's
gnawing away on a bone. They like
Jello. Found that out when I had some
earlier.

I had a dream about Grace's mom's
house last night and when I woke,
thought that something good had
happened, but it was a dream. Mandy,
however is here at Wags for the
weekend. I love her visits. She is
always so glad to see us. In that
respect, something good did happen.
It's funny that I dreamed about the
house and now Mandy is here. It was
her house too.

This has been a crazy week.
Thanksgiving week. We are booked
solid, and then some. I guess nothing in
my life has gone as I expected. No

smooth sailing up to an easy and lazy retirement. I should have read less into those stupid fairy tales. The hero and heroine were never given more than they could handle. No, they were superhuman! Nothing kept them down.

In life, real life, this is never the case. We are all given crosses to bear. Some days the crosses are lighter than others. Some days, people are introduced into your day to help you bear the weight of the cross. There is no "happily ever after" for anyone. Life is a struggle, but isn't anything that is worthwhile, worth working and fighting for? Makes us appreciate the little things.

I hate confrontation. I hate fighting unless it's for something I truly believe in. Like my relationship with Carmen, CJ and Sam. I would walk over fire for them. They piss me off, sure. It's like, it's their job. But, if someone strikes against any of my boys, you can bet your ass I'm going to react. However, when it's the three of them fighting? Ugh! I walk away.

Arguing is one thing, all out yelling is another. If a valid point is to be made, make it. Don't yell it. Then be willing to listen to someone else's opinion. Sometimes the other opinion is the correct one. No one is always right. And there are no sides. Now if I can just get this thru my boy's thick skulls and get on with business! I think we are all over worked and tired.

Thank God for the dogs. All of them. They make my life bearable. I love my sons to death, but I can't live their lives for them. They need to figure stuff out for themselves. Again, no "happily ever after". No peaceful life with no ebb and flow. Life is constantly moving and changing. Old to new. New to different. People, surroundings, everything changes. Not always for the better. Deal with it. One day at a time. One issue at a time.   How do you eat an elephant? One bite at a time!

Chapter 33

December 12, 2011

When you are given a gift, you write a thank you note to the giver. When you are given a gift from God, how do you send a thank you note? I have a natural affinity with animals, always have. I consider this a gift. When I die and the good Lord asks me what I did with this given gift, I will not pause. I took this gift and used it to the best of my ability. I did not waste my gift. I shared my talents with others. I took what has been handed to me, claimed it as my own and then decided the outcome. No one person is exempt from this. I need to be able to say, "ya know what? I had a great ride". That will be my thank you note.

Adversity is a test.   You must decide the outcome. It's up to you and no one else. I heard once that nothing makes God laugh more than when we, make plans. True. If you are showing a willingness to work and not give up, because you will be thrown obstacles, you will reach your ultimate goal.   Too many people do not persevere and they fail.

A great man, or woman, needs to fail to obtain what they were put here for in the first place. Sidebar: Over the last few years, I have found that when you rest, when you think that all is well and that you can coast, don't. Not a good idea. If you stay hungry and uncertain, you will be at the top of your game.

We went to Longboat Key again in December. It was wonderful. We decided that since we couldn't get Grace's mom's house that we would continue to live and not wait for life to happen to us. The house has a for sale sign in front of it. It's okay. Maybe it hasn't sold yet because it's waiting for us! Going to Longboat builds me back up. The sun and the warm gulf waters take the ache out of my joints and my soul.

I found out on February 14th, 2012, yes, Valentine's Day, that I have rheumatoid arthritis. So, that's what's going on! My body is betraying me and I am not happy about it! At least I have an answer and can be more proactive now in managing my health. I have to go see a rheumatologist to find out what is next for me.

So sore right now, the cold kills me. I have a warmed up corn bag on my knees. Lola is on top of that and Clark is next to me. You can't buy medicine like this. The walk this morning was brutal. We had a full house again, lots of multiples, families with two or more dogs. Walking our guests is a lot of work. CJ, his girlfriend Shelly, Sammy and I got right to it. Carmen helped also. I think he enjoyed it!

My cousin Karen's two boys, Jason and John, twins, work with us now. Eric left us to pursue a career in his chosen field. He was great to work with, but he needed to put his college degree to use. John and Jason had to miss the morning walk because of school. So glad we have a good group of guests. They are all happy to see each other and to get their business done quickly because it is cold out.

The spring and summer were crazy for us. So many dogs. And cats. And rabbits and flying squirrels, a lizard, and fish and a cockatiel. We take them all!   These last few years have been a blur. We have met some great people, and made some wonderful new friends.

Every dog adds something to our business, and to us individually. We've had some really rough times, too many to count. I've wanted to chuck it all more times than I can remember, but we hung in there and built an amazing business.

As I have said, I knew there was a need for Wags, but not to the extent. We've lost a bunch of beloved guests to old age and illness, but it seems when one dog passes, another arrives. I love them all, even the dogs that sometimes make loving them difficult.

Working with family is hard at times.   I love my boys to the moon and back, but sometimes they make me crazy. For spending as much time together at work as we do, we still enjoy spending our off time together too. I am so proud of the men that CJ and Sammy have become. They work really hard to make us great and I love that. I love to hear from customers about how well the boys handled the business while we were away. The complements make me sure that CJ and Sammy will be great when they eventually take over Wags completely.

After being diagnosed with rheumatoid arthritis, I saw a rheumatologist. I had more blood work and tests done. The rheumatologist informed me that I have osteoarthritis in my hands, carpal tunnel in my wrists, bursitis in my hips. This explains why I am so tired all the time, and so sore. I used to have so much energy!

Writing is therapy, but I do have to take frequent breaks as my hand gets really tired. The boys have really stepped up. I don't do well at all on the cold, wet days. I'd rather stay in bed. Being one that never relied on anyone to do something that I can do on my own is a real challenge too. I'm stubborn. I want things done when I want them done. I don't want to wait for anyone to do it for me. I have to learn to let stuff go. I need to understand that someone else can do a chore as well as I can. I just need to give them a chance.

Epilogue

For a time, you think that all of your life is there right in front of you, yet, you have no idea how long that will be. You think as a child, forever, but as you get older, how long, really, is forever? We are granted a certain amount of time. Some have longer than other because they have more to do. Not that - that diminishes what the others have to do, no, but sometimes it takes longer.

Sometimes we succeed, sometimes we don't. Each person is supposed to make sure that the ones that come next, make it. But, we still have to find our own way.

On August 3rd, 2012, we found our way home. By the grace of God and the love and help of a wonderful woman, we bought Grace's mom's house. It is ours, just as Grace had predicted. She tells me all the time how happy she is that we are here. I am content just to sit in my sun porch and breathe.

We occasionally see some friends from our "old" life, but the new life, and the friends that have come with it, will remain with me for life. Bonnie and Grace made us believe in people again. The friendship and encouragement freely given by them was priceless. And the hope. The will to dream.

With my family, my Mom and Dad, my siblings, and their kids, my husband and my boys, I survived the crash and burn. At times, I thought my life was over. It wasn't. It was a blessing. This has been an awesome journey that really is just beginning. No coincidences. We are exactly where we are supposed to be. I didn't count on coming out on top. It just seems to be happening that way.

I thought I lost my faith, but I didn't. My faith just matured. I thank God every day for not letting me give up. I thank God for not giving up on me. In general, I just thank God!!

With my faith came grace. Grace is a bestowal of blessings. In thinking that I knew what was best for me, I might have missed out on having Wags. Every little thing that happened in my life, has been leading to what we as a family, and a company, are becoming in this lifetime.

In order to succeed in life, one must never, never stop trying. Don't ever give up. It is so hard sometimes to think beyond today, so don't. Take the day, make it your best. And tomorrow? Do the same. Everyday. Work hard, be good to others, and have faith that you are heading in the right direction. I don't know where we would be if we had let the past run us over. I can't even fathom failure.

Keep the people you love and have your best interest at heart, close to you. Let the ones that don't, go. Surround yourself with good people. People that make you want to be better, keep them by your side as they will motivate you to reach your true potential. Love your friends for their faults, as well as, their perfections.

Each relationship adds something to who you ultimately become. If it seems like you have been given too much, step back. Really look at the mountain you perceive in your life. It will become smaller as you get closer to it. Before you even realize it, you will be on the mountain's top. You haven't heard the last of me yet! Wag on!!!

About the Author

Anne Mallore feels writing "about the author" is like writing her obituary. Speaking in the third person is one of her pet peeves. However, she will give it a whirl.

Anne Mallore is an author and owner of Wags Pet Center in Marcellus, New York. She and her husband, Carmen have been delightfully married for thirty-two years. They are blessed with two sons, CJ and Sammy that are the joy of their lives. She lives in her forever home in Camillus, New York with her husband Carmen, and their two shih-tzus, Lola and Clark.

Anne is currently working on a second book about some of the guests from Wags. Anne is inspired by the animals she has met along her life's journey, and by the special bonds formed along the way. She is looking forward to going back to Longboat, as it is always on her mind. Connect with Anne at Livelaughwag22@gmail.com & Facebook

43310972R00153

Made in the USA
Lexington, KY
25 July 2015